C-2224 | **CAREER EXAMINATION SERIES**

THIS IS YOUR PASSBOOK® FOR ...
WATER METER READER

COPYRIGHT NOTICE

This book is SOLELY intended for, is sold ONLY to, and its use is RESTRICTED to individual, bona fide applicants or candidates who qualify by virtue of having seriously filed applications for appropriate license, certificate, professional and/or promotional advancement, higher school matriculation, scholarship, or other legitimate requirements of educational and/or governmental authorities.

This book is NOT intended for use, class instruction, tutoring, training, duplication, copying, reprinting, excerption, or adaptation, etc., by:

1) Other publishers
2) Proprietors and/or Instructors of «Coaching» and/or Preparatory Courses
3) Personnel and/or Training Divisions of commercial, industrial, and governmental organizations
4) Schools, colleges, or universities and/or their departments and staffs, including teachers and other personnel
5) Testing Agencies or Bureaus
6) Study groups which seek by the purchase of a single volume to copy and/or duplicate and/or adapt this material for use by the group as a whole without having purchased individual volumes for each of the members of the group
7) Et al.

Such persons would be in violation of appropriate Federal and State statutes.

PROVISION OF LICENSING AGREEMENTS. — Recognized educational, commercial, industrial, and governmental institutions and organizations, and others legitimately engaged in educational pursuits, including training, testing, and measurement activities, may address request for a licensing agreement to the copyright owners, who will determine whether, and under what conditions, including fees and charges, the materials in this book may be used them. In other words, a licensing facility exists for the legitimate use of the material in this book on other than an individual basis. However, it is asseverated and affirmed here that the material in this book CANNOT be used without the receipt of the express permission of such a licensing agreement from the Publishers. Inquiries re licensing should be addressed to the company, attention rights and permissions department.

All rights reserved, including the right of reproduction in whole or in part, in any form or by any means, electronic or mechanical, including photocopying, recording, or by any information storage and retrieval system, without permission in writing from the Publisher.

Copyright © 2018 by

NLC®

National Learning Corporation

212 Michael Drive, Syosset, NY 11791
(516) 921-8888 • www.passbooks.com
E-mail: info@passbooks.com

PUBLISHED IN THE UNITED STATES OF AMERICA

PASSBOOK® SERIES

THE *PASSBOOK® SERIES* has been created to prepare applicants and candidates for the ultimate academic battlefield – the examination room.

At some time in our lives, each and every one of us may be required to take an examination – for validation, matriculation, admission, qualification, registration, certification, or licensure.

Based on the assumption that every applicant or candidate has met the basic formal educational standards, has taken the required number of courses, and read the necessary texts, the *PASSBOOK® SERIES* furnishes the one special preparation which may assure passing with confidence, instead of failing with insecurity. Examination questions – together with answers – are furnished as the basic vehicle for study so that the mysteries of the examination and its compounding difficulties may be eliminated or diminished by a sure method.

This book is meant to help you pass your examination provided that you qualify and are serious in your objective.

The entire field is reviewed through the huge store of content information which is succinctly presented through a provocative and challenging approach – the question-and-answer method.

A climate of success is established by furnishing the correct answers at the end of each test.

You soon learn to recognize types of questions, forms of questions, and patterns of questioning. You may even begin to anticipate expected outcomes.

You perceive that many questions are repeated or adapted so that you can gain acute insights, which may enable you to score many sure points.

You learn how to confront new questions, or types of questions, and to attack them confidently and work out the correct answers.

You note objectives and emphases, and recognize pitfalls and dangers, so that you may make positive educational adjustments.

Moreover, you are kept fully informed in relation to new concepts, methods, practices, and directions in the field.

You discover that you arre actually taking the examination all the time: you are preparing for the examination by "taking" an examination, not by reading extraneous and/or supererogatory textbooks.

In short, this PASSBOOK®, used directedly, should be an important factor in helping you to pass your test.

WATER METER READER

DUTIES AND RESPONSIBILITIES
Under supervision, performs routine tasks of ordinary difficulty and responsibility in reporting water consumption, insuring conformance to rules, standards, and regulations of the department related to water meters and assisting in other field or office programs involving water consumption; performs related work.

EXAMPLES OF TYPICAL TASKS
Reads water meters. May verify water meter readings. Computes the water consumed since the last reading and compares it with similar periods to detect possible waste. Reports violations of department rules and regulations. Tests meter to insure that water consumption is registered on the meter. Accompanies inspectors in the field, receives on-the-job training and assists in the performance of routine tasks. Prepares reports requiring simple mathematical computations.

TESTS
The written test will be of the multiple-choice type and may include questions on ability to read water meters; ability to make arithmetic calculations; reading comprehension; name and number checking; public relations; safety; and other related areas.

HOW TO TAKE A TEST

I. YOU MUST PASS AN EXAMINATION

A. *WHAT EVERY CANDIDATE SHOULD KNOW*

Examination applicants often ask us for help in preparing for the written test. What can I study in advance? What kinds of questions will be asked? How will the test be given? How will the papers be graded?

As an applicant for a civil service examination, you may be wondering about some of these things. Our purpose here is to suggest effective methods of advance study and to describe civil service examinations.

Your chances for success on this examination can be increased if you know how to prepare. Those "pre-examination jitters" can be reduced if you know what to expect. You can even experience an adventure in good citizenship if you know why civil service exams are given.

B. *WHY ARE CIVIL SERVICE EXAMINATIONS GIVEN?*

Civil service examinations are important to you in two ways. As a citizen, you want public jobs filled by employees who know how to do their work. As a job seeker, you want a fair chance to compete for that job on an equal footing with other candidates. The best-known means of accomplishing this two-fold goal is the competitive examination.

Exams are widely publicized throughout the nation. They may be administered for jobs in federal, state, city, municipal, town or village governments or agencies.

Any citizen may apply, with some limitations, such as the age or residence of applicants. Your experience and education may be reviewed to see whether you meet the requirements for the particular examination. When these requirements exist, they are reasonable and applied consistently to all applicants. Thus, a competitive examination may cause you some uneasiness now, but it is your privilege and safeguard.

C. *HOW ARE CIVIL SERVICE EXAMS DEVELOPED?*

Examinations are carefully written by trained technicians who are specialists in the field known as "psychological measurement," in consultation with recognized authorities in the field of work that the test will cover. These experts recommend the subject matter areas or skills to be tested; only those knowledges or skills important to your success on the job are included. The most reliable books and source materials available are used as references. Together, the experts and technicians judge the difficulty level of the questions.

Test technicians know how to phrase questions so that the problem is clearly stated. Their ethics do not permit "trick" or "catch" questions. Questions may have been tried out on sample groups, or subjected to statistical analysis, to determine their usefulness.

Written tests are often used in combination with performance tests, ratings of training and experience, and oral interviews. All of these measures combine to form the best-known means of finding the right person for the right job.

II. HOW TO PASS THE WRITTEN TEST

A. NATURE OF THE EXAMINATION

To prepare intelligently for civil service examinations, you should know how they differ from school examinations you have taken. In school you were assigned certain definite pages to read or subjects to cover. The examination questions were quite detailed and usually emphasized memory. Civil service exams, on the other hand, try to discover your present ability to perform the duties of a position, plus your potentiality to learn these duties. In other words, a civil service exam attempts to predict how successful you will be. Questions cover such a broad area that they cannot be as minute and detailed as school exam questions.

In the public service similar kinds of work, or positions, are grouped together in one "class." This process is known as *position-classification*. All the positions in a class are paid according to the salary range for that class. One class title covers all of these positions, and they are all tested by the same examination.

B. FOUR BASIC STEPS

1) Study the announcement

How, then, can you know what subjects to study? Our best answer is: "Learn as much as possible about the class of positions for which you've applied." The exam will test the knowledge, skills and abilities needed to do the work.

Your most valuable source of information about the position you want is the official exam announcement. This announcement lists the training and experience qualifications. Check these standards and apply only if you come reasonably close to meeting them.

The brief description of the position in the examination announcement offers some clues to the subjects which will be tested. Think about the job itself. Review the duties in your mind. Can you perform them, or are there some in which you are rusty? Fill in the blank spots in your preparation.

Many jurisdictions preview the written test in the exam announcement by including a section called "Knowledge and Abilities Required," "Scope of the Examination," or some similar heading. Here you will find out specifically what fields will be tested.

2) Review your own background

Once you learn in general what the position is all about, and what you need to know to do the work, ask yourself which subjects you already know fairly well and which need improvement. You may wonder whether to concentrate on improving your strong areas or on building some background in your fields of weakness. When the announcement has specified "some knowledge" or "considerable knowledge," or has used adjectives like "beginning principles of…" or "advanced … methods," you can get a clue as to the number and difficulty of questions to be asked in any given field. More questions, and hence broader coverage, would be included for those subjects which are more important in the work. Now weigh your strengths and weaknesses against the job requirements and prepare accordingly.

3) Determine the level of the position

Another way to tell how intensively you should prepare is to understand the level of the job for which you are applying. Is it the entering level? In other words, is this the position in which beginners in a field of work are hired? Or is it an intermediate or advanced level? Sometimes this is indicated by such words as "Junior" or "Senior" in the class title. Other jurisdictions use Roman numerals to designate the level – Clerk I, Clerk II, for example. The word "Supervisor" sometimes appears in the title. If the level is not indicated by the title, check the description of duties. Will you be working under very close supervision, or will you have responsibility for independent decisions in this work?

4) Choose appropriate study materials

Now that you know the subjects to be examined and the relative amount of each subject to be covered, you can choose suitable study materials. For beginning level jobs, or even advanced ones, if you have a pronounced weakness in some aspect of your training, read a modern, standard textbook in that field. Be sure it is up to date and has general coverage. Such books are normally available at your library, and the librarian will be glad to help you locate one. For entry-level positions, questions of appropriate difficulty are chosen – neither highly advanced questions, nor those too simple. Such questions require careful thought but not advanced training.

If the position for which you are applying is technical or advanced, you will read more advanced, specialized material. If you are already familiar with the basic principles of your field, elementary textbooks would waste your time. Concentrate on advanced textbooks and technical periodicals. Think through the concepts and review difficult problems in your field.

These are all general sources. You can get more ideas on your own initiative, following these leads. For example, training manuals and publications of the government agency which employs workers in your field can be useful, particularly for technical and professional positions. A letter or visit to the government department involved may result in more specific study suggestions, and certainly will provide you with a more definite idea of the exact nature of the position you are seeking.

III. KINDS OF TESTS

Tests are used for purposes other than measuring knowledge and ability to perform specified duties. For some positions, it is equally important to test ability to make adjustments to new situations or to profit from training. In others, basic mental abilities not dependent on information are essential. Questions which test these things may not appear as pertinent to the duties of the position as those which test for knowledge and information. Yet they are often highly important parts of a fair examination. For very general questions, it is almost impossible to help you direct your study efforts. What we can do is to point out some of the more common of these general abilities needed in public service positions and describe some typical questions.

1) General information

Broad, general information has been found useful for predicting job success in some kinds of work. This is tested in a variety of ways, from vocabulary lists to questions about current events. Basic background in some field of work, such as sociology or economics, may be sampled in a group of questions. Often these are principles which have become familiar to most persons through exposure rather than through formal training. It is difficult to advise you how to study for these questions; being alert to the world around you is our best suggestion.

2) Verbal ability

An example of an ability needed in many positions is verbal or language ability. Verbal ability is, in brief, the ability to use and understand words. Vocabulary and grammar tests are typical measures of this ability. Reading comprehension or paragraph interpretation questions are common in many kinds of civil service tests. You are given a paragraph of written material and asked to find its central meaning.

3) Numerical ability

Number skills can be tested by the familiar arithmetic problem, by checking paired lists of numbers to see which are alike and which are different, or by interpreting charts and graphs. In the latter test, a graph may be printed in the test booklet which you are asked to use as the basis for answering questions.

4) Observation

A popular test for law-enforcement positions is the observation test. A picture is shown to you for several minutes, then taken away. Questions about the picture test your ability to observe both details and larger elements.

5) Following directions

In many positions in the public service, the employee must be able to carry out written instructions dependably and accurately. You may be given a chart with several columns, each column listing a variety of information. The questions require you to carry out directions involving the information given in the chart.

6) Skills and aptitudes

Performance tests effectively measure some manual skills and aptitudes. When the skill is one in which you are trained, such as typing or shorthand, you can practice. These tests are often very much like those given in business school or high school courses. For many of the other skills and aptitudes, however, no short-time preparation can be made. Skills and abilities natural to you or that you have developed throughout your lifetime are being tested.

Many of the general questions just described provide all the data needed to answer the questions and ask you to use your reasoning ability to find the answers. Your best preparation for these tests, as well as for tests of facts and ideas, is to be at your physical and mental best. You, no doubt, have your own methods of getting into an exam-taking mood and keeping "in shape." The next section lists some ideas on this subject.

IV. KINDS OF QUESTIONS

Only rarely is the "essay" question, which you answer in narrative form, used in civil service tests. Civil service tests are usually of the short-answer type. Full instructions for answering these questions will be given to you at the examination. But in case this is your first experience with short-answer questions and separate answer sheets, here is what you need to know:

1) Multiple-choice Questions

Most popular of the short-answer questions is the "multiple choice" or "best answer" question. It can be used, for example, to test for factual knowledge, ability to solve problems or judgment in meeting situations found at work.

A multiple-choice question is normally one of three types—

- It can begin with an incomplete statement followed by several possible endings. You are to find the one ending which *best* completes the statement, although some of the others may not be entirely wrong.
- It can also be a complete statement in the form of a question which is answered by choosing one of the statements listed.
- It can be in the form of a problem – again you select the best answer.

Here is an example of a multiple-choice question with a discussion which should give you some clues as to the method for choosing the right answer:

When an employee has a complaint about his assignment, the action which will *best* help him overcome his difficulty is to
   A. discuss his difficulty with his coworkers
   B. take the problem to the head of the organization
   C. take the problem to the person who gave him the assignment
   D. say nothing to anyone about his complaint

In answering this question, you should study each of the choices to find which is best. Consider choice "A" – Certainly an employee may discuss his complaint with fellow employees, but no change or improvement can result, and the complaint remains unresolved. Choice "B" is a poor choice since the head of the organization probably does not know what assignment you have been given, and taking your problem to him is known as "going over the head" of the supervisor. The supervisor, or person who made the assignment, is the person who can clarify it or correct any injustice. Choice "C" is, therefore, correct. To say nothing, as in choice "D," is unwise. Supervisors have and interest in knowing the problems employees are facing, and the employee is seeking a solution to his problem.

2) True/False Questions

The "true/false" or "right/wrong" form of question is sometimes used. Here a complete statement is given. Your job is to decide whether the statement is right or wrong.

SAMPLE: A roaming cell-phone call to a nearby city costs less than a non-roaming call to a distant city.

This statement is wrong, or false, since roaming calls are more expensive.
This is not a complete list of all possible question forms, although most of the others are variations of these common types. You will always get complete directions for

answering questions. Be sure you understand *how* to mark your answers – ask questions until you do.

V. RECORDING YOUR ANSWERS

Computer terminals are used more and more today for many different kinds of exams.

For an examination with very few applicants, you may be told to record your answers in the test booklet itself. Separate answer sheets are much more common. If this separate answer sheet is to be scored by machine – and this is often the case – it is highly important that you mark your answers correctly in order to get credit.

An electronic scoring machine is often used in civil service offices because of the speed with which papers can be scored. Machine-scored answer sheets must be marked with a pencil, which will be given to you. This pencil has a high graphite content which responds to the electronic scoring machine. As a matter of fact, stray dots may register as answers, so do not let your pencil rest on the answer sheet while you are pondering the correct answer. Also, if your pencil lead breaks or is otherwise defective, ask for another.

Since the answer sheet will be dropped in a slot in the scoring machine, be careful not to bend the corners or get the paper crumpled.

The answer sheet normally has five vertical columns of numbers, with 30 numbers to a column. These numbers correspond to the question numbers in your test booklet. After each number, going across the page are four or five pairs of dotted lines. These short dotted lines have small letters or numbers above them. The first two pairs may also have a "T" or "F" above the letters. This indicates that the first two pairs only are to be used if the questions are of the true-false type. If the questions are multiple choice, disregard the "T" and "F" and pay attention only to the small letters or numbers.

Answer your questions in the manner of the sample that follows:

32. The largest city in the United States is
    A. Washington, D.C.
    B. New York City
    C. Chicago
    D. Detroit
    E. San Francisco

1) Choose the answer you think is best. (New York City is the largest, so "B" is correct.)
2) Find the row of dotted lines numbered the same as the question you are answering. (Find row number 32)
3) Find the pair of dotted lines corresponding to the answer. (Find the pair of lines under the mark "B.")
4) Make a solid black mark between the dotted lines.

VI. BEFORE THE TEST

Common sense will help you find procedures to follow to get ready for an examination. Too many of us, however, overlook these sensible measures. Indeed, nervousness and fatigue have been found to be the most serious reasons why applicants fail to do their best on civil service tests. Here is a list of reminders:

- Begin your preparation early – Don't wait until the last minute to go scurrying around for books and materials or to find out what the position is all about.
- Prepare continuously – An hour a night for a week is better than an all-night cram session. This has been definitely established. What is more, a night a week for a month will return better dividends than crowding your study into a shorter period of time.
- Locate the place of the exam – You have been sent a notice telling you when and where to report for the examination. If the location is in a different town or otherwise unfamiliar to you, it would be well to inquire the best route and learn something about the building.
- Relax the night before the test – Allow your mind to rest. Do not study at all that night. Plan some mild recreation or diversion; then go to bed early and get a good night's sleep.
- Get up early enough to make a leisurely trip to the place for the test – This way unforeseen events, traffic snarls, unfamiliar buildings, etc. will not upset you.
- Dress comfortably – A written test is not a fashion show. You will be known by number and not by name, so wear something comfortable.
- Leave excess paraphernalia at home – Shopping bags and odd bundles will get in your way. You need bring only the items mentioned in the official notice you received; usually everything you need is provided. Do not bring reference books to the exam. They will only confuse those last minutes and be taken away from you when in the test room.
- Arrive somewhat ahead of time – If because of transportation schedules you must get there very early, bring a newspaper or magazine to take your mind off yourself while waiting.
- Locate the examination room – When you have found the proper room, you will be directed to the seat or part of the room where you will sit. Sometimes you are given a sheet of instructions to read while you are waiting. Do not fill out any forms until you are told to do so; just read them and be prepared.
- Relax and prepare to listen to the instructions
- If you have any physical problem that may keep you from doing your best, be sure to tell the test administrator. If you are sick or in poor health, you really cannot do your best on the exam. You can come back and take the test some other time.

VII. AT THE TEST

The day of the test is here and you have the test booklet in your hand. The temptation to get going is very strong. Caution! There is more to success than knowing the right answers. You must know how to identify your papers and understand variations in the type of short-answer question used in this particular examination. Follow these suggestions for maximum results from your efforts:

1) Cooperate with the monitor

The test administrator has a duty to create a situation in which you can be as much at ease as possible. He will give instructions, tell you when to begin, check to see that you are marking your answer sheet correctly, and so on. He is not there to guard you, although he will see that your competitors do not take unfair advantage. He wants to help you do your best.

2) Listen to all instructions

Don't jump the gun! Wait until you understand all directions. In most civil service tests you get more time than you need to answer the questions. So don't be in a hurry. Read each word of instructions until you clearly understand the meaning. Study the examples, listen to all announcements and follow directions. Ask questions if you do not understand what to do.

3) Identify your papers

Civil service exams are usually identified by number only. You will be assigned a number; you must not put your name on your test papers. Be sure to copy your number correctly. Since more than one exam may be given, copy your exact examination title.

4) Plan your time

Unless you are told that a test is a "speed" or "rate of work" test, speed itself is usually not important. Time enough to answer all the questions will be provided, but this does not mean that you have all day. An overall time limit has been set. Divide the total time (in minutes) by the number of questions to determine the approximate time you have for each question.

5) Do not linger over difficult questions

If you come across a difficult question, mark it with a paper clip (useful to have along) and come back to it when you have been through the booklet. One caution if you do this – be sure to skip a number on your answer sheet as well. Check often to be sure that you have not lost your place and that you are marking in the row numbered the same as the question you are answering.

6) Read the questions

Be sure you know what the question asks! Many capable people are unsuccessful because they failed to *read* the questions correctly.

7) Answer all questions

Unless you have been instructed that a penalty will be deducted for incorrect answers, it is better to guess than to omit a question.

8) Speed tests

It is often better NOT to guess on speed tests. It has been found that on timed tests people are tempted to spend the last few seconds before time is called in marking answers at random – without even reading them – in the hope of picking up a few extra points. To discourage this practice, the instructions may warn you that your score will be "corrected" for guessing. That is, a penalty will be applied. The incorrect answers will be deducted from the correct ones, or some other penalty formula will be used.

9) Review your answers

If you finish before time is called, go back to the questions you guessed or omitted to give them further thought. Review other answers if you have time.

10) Return your test materials

If you are ready to leave before others have finished or time is called, take ALL your materials to the monitor and leave quietly. Never take any test material with you. The monitor can discover whose papers are not complete, and taking a test booklet may be grounds for disqualification.

VIII. EXAMINATION TECHNIQUES

1) Read the general instructions carefully. These are usually printed on the first page of the exam booklet. As a rule, these instructions refer to the timing of the examination; the fact that you should not start work until the signal and must stop work at a signal, etc. If there are any *special* instructions, such as a choice of questions to be answered, make sure that you note this instruction carefully.

2) When you are ready to start work on the examination, that is as soon as the signal has been given, read the instructions to each question booklet, underline any key words or phrases, such as *least*, *best*, *outline*, *describe* and the like. In this way you will tend to answer as requested rather than discover on reviewing your paper that you *listed without describing*, that you selected the *worst* choice rather than the *best* choice, etc.

3) If the examination is of the objective or multiple-choice type – that is, each question will also give a series of possible answers: A, B, C or D, and you are called upon to select the best answer and write the letter next to that answer on your answer paper – it is advisable to start answering each question in turn. There may be anywhere from 50 to 100 such questions in the three or four hours allotted and you can see how much time would be taken if you read through all the questions before beginning to answer any. Furthermore, if you come across a question or group of questions which you know would be difficult to answer, it would undoubtedly affect your handling of all the other questions.

4) If the examination is of the essay type and contains but a few questions, it is a moot point as to whether you should read all the questions before starting to answer any one. Of course, if you are given a choice – say five out of seven and the like – then it is essential to read all the questions so you can eliminate the two that are most difficult. If, however, you are asked to answer all the questions, there may be danger in trying to answer the easiest one first because you may find that you will spend too much time on it. The best technique is to answer the first question, then proceed to the second, etc.

5) Time your answers. Before the exam begins, write down the time it started, then add the time allowed for the examination and write down the time it must be completed, then divide the time available somewhat as follows:

- If 3-1/2 hours are allowed, that would be 210 minutes. If you have 80 objective-type questions, that would be an average of 2-1/2 minutes per question. Allow yourself no more than 2 minutes per question, or a total of 160 minutes, which will permit about 50 minutes to review.
- If for the time allotment of 210 minutes there are 7 essay questions to answer, that would average about 30 minutes a question. Give yourself only 25 minutes per question so that you have about 35 minutes to review.

6) The most important instruction is to *read each question* and make sure you know what is wanted. The second most important instruction is to *time yourself properly* so that you answer every question. The third most important instruction is to *answer every question*. Guess if you have to but include something for each question. Remember that you will receive no credit for a blank and will probably receive some credit if you write something in answer to an essay question. If you guess a letter – say "B" for a multiple-choice question – you may have guessed right. If you leave a blank as an answer to a multiple-choice question, the examiners may respect your feelings but it will not add a point to your score. Some exams may penalize you for wrong answers, so in such cases *only*, you may not want to guess unless you have some basis for your answer.

7) Suggestions
   a. Objective-type questions
      1. Examine the question booklet for proper sequence of pages and questions
      2. Read all instructions carefully
      3. Skip any question which seems too difficult; return to it after all other questions have been answered
      4. Apportion your time properly; do not spend too much time on any single question or group of questions
      5. Note and underline key words – *all, most, fewest, least, best, worst, same, opposite,* etc.
      6. Pay particular attention to negatives
      7. Note unusual option, e.g., unduly long, short, complex, different or similar in content to the body of the question
      8. Observe the use of "hedging" words – *probably, may, most likely,* etc.
      9. Make sure that your answer is put next to the same number as the question
      10. Do not second-guess unless you have good reason to believe the second answer is definitely more correct
      11. Cross out original answer if you decide another answer is more accurate; do not erase until you are ready to hand your paper in
      12. Answer all questions; guess unless instructed otherwise
      13. Leave time for review

   b. Essay questions
      1. Read each question carefully
      2. Determine exactly what is wanted. Underline key words or phrases.
      3. Decide on outline or paragraph answer

4. Include many different points and elements unless asked to develop any one or two points or elements
5. Show impartiality by giving pros and cons unless directed to select one side only
6. Make and write down any assumptions you find necessary to answer the questions
7. Watch your English, grammar, punctuation and choice of words
8. Time your answers; don't crowd material

8) Answering the essay question

Most essay questions can be answered by framing the specific response around several key words or ideas. Here are a few such key words or ideas:

M's: manpower, materials, methods, money, management
P's: purpose, program, policy, plan, procedure, practice, problems, pitfalls, personnel, public relations

  a. Six basic steps in handling problems:
    1. Preliminary plan and background development
    2. Collect information, data and facts
    3. Analyze and interpret information, data and facts
    4. Analyze and develop solutions as well as make recommendations
    5. Prepare report and sell recommendations
    6. Install recommendations and follow up effectiveness

  b. Pitfalls to avoid
    1. *Taking things for granted* – A statement of the situation does not necessarily imply that each of the elements is necessarily true; for example, a complaint may be invalid and biased so that all that can be taken for granted is that a complaint has been registered
    2. *Considering only one side of a situation* – Wherever possible, indicate several alternatives and then point out the reasons you selected the best one
    3. *Failing to indicate follow up* – Whenever your answer indicates action on your part, make certain that you will take proper follow-up action to see how successful your recommendations, procedures or actions turn out to be
    4. *Taking too long in answering any single question* – Remember to time your answers properly

IX. AFTER THE TEST

Scoring procedures differ in detail among civil service jurisdictions although the general principles are the same. Whether the papers are hand-scored or graded by machine we have described, they are nearly always graded by number. That is, the person who marks the paper knows only the number – never the name – of the applicant. Not until all the papers have been graded will they be matched with names. If other tests, such as training and experience or oral interview ratings have been given, scores will be combined. Different parts of the examination usually have different weights. For example, the written test might count 60 percent of the final grade, and a rating of training and experience 40 percent. In many jurisdictions, veterans will have a certain number of points added to their grades.

After the final grade has been determined, the names are placed in grade order and an eligible list is established. There are various methods for resolving ties between those who get the same final grade – probably the most common is to place first the name of the person whose application was received first. Job offers are made from the eligible list in the order the names appear on it. You will be notified of your grade and your rank as soon as all these computations have been made. This will be done as rapidly as possible.

People who are found to meet the requirements in the announcement are called "eligibles." Their names are put on a list of eligible candidates. An eligible's chances of getting a job depend on how high he stands on this list and how fast agencies are filling jobs from the list.

When a job is to be filled from a list of eligibles, the agency asks for the names of people on the list of eligibles for that job. When the civil service commission receives this request, it sends to the agency the names of the three people highest on this list. Or, if the job to be filled has specialized requirements, the office sends the agency the names of the top three persons who meet these requirements from the general list.

The appointing officer makes a choice from among the three people whose names were sent to him. If the selected person accepts the appointment, the names of the others are put back on the list to be considered for future openings.

That is the rule in hiring from all kinds of eligible lists, whether they are for typist, carpenter, chemist, or something else. For every vacancy, the appointing officer has his choice of any one of the top three eligibles on the list. This explains why the person whose name is on top of the list sometimes does not get an appointment when some of the persons lower on the list do. If the appointing officer chooses the second or third eligible, the No. 1 eligible does not get a job at once, but stays on the list until he is appointed or the list is terminated.

X. HOW TO PASS THE INTERVIEW TEST

The examination for which you applied requires an oral interview test. You have already taken the written test and you are now being called for the interview test – the final part of the formal examination.

You may think that it is not possible to prepare for an interview test and that there are no procedures to follow during an interview. Our purpose is to point out some things you can do in advance that will help you and some good rules to follow and pitfalls to avoid while you are being interviewed.

What is an interview supposed to test?

The written examination is designed to test the technical knowledge and competence of the candidate; the oral is designed to evaluate intangible qualities, not readily measured otherwise, and to establish a list showing the relative fitness of each candidate – as measured against his competitors – for the position sought. Scoring is not on the basis of "right" and "wrong," but on a sliding scale of values ranging from "not passable" to "outstanding." As a matter of fact, it is possible to achieve a relatively low score without a single "incorrect" answer because of evident weakness in the qualities being measured.

Occasionally, an examination may consist entirely of an oral test – either an individual or a group oral. In such cases, information is sought concerning the technical knowledges and abilities of the candidate, since there has been no written examination for this purpose. More commonly, however, an oral test is used to supplement a written examination.

Who conducts interviews?
The composition of oral boards varies among different jurisdictions. In nearly all, a representative of the personnel department serves as chairman. One of the members of the board may be a representative of the department in which the candidate would work. In some cases, "outside experts" are used, and, frequently, a businessman or some other representative of the general public is asked to serve. Labor and management or other special groups may be represented. The aim is to secure the services of experts in the appropriate field.

However the board is composed, it is a good idea (and not at all improper or unethical) to ascertain in advance of the interview who the members are and what groups they represent. When you are introduced to them, you will have some idea of their backgrounds and interests, and at least you will not stutter and stammer over their names.

What should be done before the interview?
While knowledge about the board members is useful and takes some of the surprise element out of the interview, there is other preparation which is more substantive. It *is* possible to prepare for an oral interview – in several ways:

1) Keep a copy of your application and review it carefully before the interview
This may be the only document before the oral board, and the starting point of the interview. Know what education and experience you have listed there, and the sequence and dates of all of it. Sometimes the board will ask you to review the highlights of your experience for them; you should not have to hem and haw doing it.

2) Study the class specification and the examination announcement
Usually, the oral board has one or both of these to guide them. The qualities, characteristics or knowledges required by the position sought are stated in these documents. They offer valuable clues as to the nature of the oral interview. For example, if the job involves supervisory responsibilities, the announcement will usually indicate that knowledge of modern supervisory methods and the qualifications of the candidate as a supervisor will be tested. If so, you can expect such questions, frequently in the form of a hypothetical situation which you are expected to solve. NEVER go into an oral without knowledge of the duties and responsibilities of the job you seek.

3) Think through each qualification required
Try to visualize the kind of questions you would ask if you were a board member. How well could you answer them? Try especially to appraise your own knowledge and background in each area, *measured against the job sought*, and identify any areas in which you are weak. Be critical and realistic – do not flatter yourself.

4) Do some general reading in areas in which you feel you may be weak
For example, if the job involves supervision and your past experience has NOT, some general reading in supervisory methods and practices, particularly in the field of human relations, might be useful. Do NOT study agency procedures or detailed manuals. The oral board will be testing your understanding and capacity, not your memory.

5) Get a good night's sleep and watch your general health and mental attitude
You will want a clear head at the interview. Take care of a cold or any other minor ailment, and of course, no hangovers.

What should be done on the day of the interview?
Now comes the day of the interview itself. Give yourself plenty of time to get there. Plan to arrive somewhat ahead of the scheduled time, particularly if your appointment is in the fore part of the day. If a previous candidate fails to appear, the board might be ready for you a bit early. By early afternoon an oral board is almost invariably behind schedule if there are many candidates, and you may have to wait. Take along a book or magazine to read, or your application to review, but leave any extraneous material in the waiting room when you go in for your interview. In any event, relax and compose yourself.

The matter of dress is important. The board is forming impressions about you – from your experience, your manners, your attitude, and your appearance. Give your personal appearance careful attention. Dress your best, but not your flashiest. Choose conservative, appropriate clothing, and be sure it is immaculate. This is a business interview, and your appearance should indicate that you regard it as such. Besides, being well groomed and properly dressed will help boost your confidence.

Sooner or later, someone will call your name and escort you into the interview room. *This is it.* From here on you are on your own. It is too late for any more preparation. But remember, you asked for this opportunity to prove your fitness, and you are here because your request was granted.

What happens when you go in?
The usual sequence of events will be as follows: The clerk (who is often the board stenographer) will introduce you to the chairman of the oral board, who will introduce you to the other members of the board. Acknowledge the introductions before you sit down. Do not be surprised if you find a microphone facing you or a stenotypist sitting by. Oral interviews are usually recorded in the event of an appeal or other review.

Usually the chairman of the board will open the interview by reviewing the highlights of your education and work experience from your application – primarily for the benefit of the other members of the board, as well as to get the material into the record. Do not interrupt or comment unless there is an error or significant misinterpretation; if that is the case, do not hesitate. But do not quibble about insignificant matters. Also, he will usually ask you some question about your education, experience or your present job – partly to get you to start talking and to establish the interviewing "rapport." He may start the actual questioning, or turn it over to one of the other members. Frequently, each member undertakes the questioning on a particular area, one in which he is perhaps most competent, so you can expect each member to participate in the examination. Because time is limited, you may also expect some rather abrupt switches in the direction the questioning takes, so do not be upset by it. Normally, a board member will not pursue a single line of questioning unless he discovers a particular strength or weakness.

After each member has participated, the chairman will usually ask whether any member has any further questions, then will ask you if you have anything you wish to add. Unless you are expecting this question, it may floor you. Worse, it may start you off on an extended, extemporaneous speech. The board is not usually seeking more information. The question is principally to offer you a last opportunity to present further qualifications or to indicate that you have nothing to add. So, if you feel that a significant qualification or characteristic has been overlooked, it is proper to point it out in a sentence or so. Do not compliment the board on the thoroughness of their examination – they have been sketchy, and you know it. If you wish, merely say, "No thank you, I have nothing further to add." This is a point where you can "talk yourself out" of a good impression or fail to present an important bit of information. Remember, *you close the interview yourself.*

The chairman will then say, "That is all, Mr. _____, thank you." Do not be startled; the interview is over, and quicker than you think. Thank him, gather your belongings and take your leave. Save your sigh of relief for the other side of the door.

How to put your best foot forward

Throughout this entire process, you may feel that the board individually and collectively is trying to pierce your defenses, seek out your hidden weaknesses and embarrass and confuse you. Actually, this is not true. They are obliged to make an appraisal of your qualifications for the job you are seeking, and they want to see you in your best light. Remember, they must interview all candidates and a non-cooperative candidate may become a failure in spite of their best efforts to bring out his qualifications. Here are 15 suggestions that will help you:

1) Be natural – Keep your attitude confident, not cocky

If you are not confident that you can do the job, do not expect the board to be. Do not apologize for your weaknesses, try to bring out your strong points. The board is interested in a positive, not negative, presentation. Cockiness will antagonize any board member and make him wonder if you are covering up a weakness by a false show of strength.

2) Get comfortable, but don't lounge or sprawl

Sit erectly but not stiffly. A careless posture may lead the board to conclude that you are careless in other things, or at least that you are not impressed by the importance of the occasion. Either conclusion is natural, even if incorrect. Do not fuss with your clothing, a pencil or an ashtray. Your hands may occasionally be useful to emphasize a point; do not let them become a point of distraction.

3) Do not wisecrack or make small talk

This is a serious situation, and your attitude should show that you consider it as such. Further, the time of the board is limited – they do not want to waste it, and neither should you.

4) Do not exaggerate your experience or abilities

In the first place, from information in the application or other interviews and sources, the board may know more about you than you think. Secondly, you probably will not get away with it. An experienced board is rather adept at spotting such a situation, so do not take the chance.

5) If you know a board member, do not make a point of it, yet do not hide it
Certainly you are not fooling him, and probably not the other members of the board. Do not try to take advantage of your acquaintanceship – it will probably do you little good.

6) Do not dominate the interview
Let the board do that. They will give you the clues – do not assume that you have to do all the talking. Realize that the board has a number of questions to ask you, and do not try to take up all the interview time by showing off your extensive knowledge of the answer to the first one.

7) Be attentive
You only have 20 minutes or so, and you should keep your attention at its sharpest throughout. When a member is addressing a problem or question to you, give him your undivided attention. Address your reply principally to him, but do not exclude the other board members.

8) Do not interrupt
A board member may be stating a problem for you to analyze. He will ask you a question when the time comes. Let him state the problem, and wait for the question.

9) Make sure you understand the question
Do not try to answer until you are sure what the question is. If it is not clear, restate it in your own words or ask the board member to clarify it for you. However, do not haggle about minor elements.

10) Reply promptly but not hastily
A common entry on oral board rating sheets is "candidate responded readily," or "candidate hesitated in replies." Respond as promptly and quickly as you can, but do not jump to a hasty, ill-considered answer.

11) Do not be peremptory in your answers
A brief answer is proper – but do not fire your answer back. That is a losing game from your point of view. The board member can probably ask questions much faster than you can answer them.

12) Do not try to create the answer you think the board member wants
He is interested in what kind of mind you have and how it works – not in playing games. Furthermore, he can usually spot this practice and will actually grade you down on it.

13) Do not switch sides in your reply merely to agree with a board member
Frequently, a member will take a contrary position merely to draw you out and to see if you are willing and able to defend your point of view. Do not start a debate, yet do not surrender a good position. If a position is worth taking, it is worth defending.

14) Do not be afraid to admit an error in judgment if you are shown to be wrong

The board knows that you are forced to reply without any opportunity for careful consideration. Your answer may be demonstrably wrong. If so, admit it and get on with the interview.

15) Do not dwell at length on your present job

The opening question may relate to your present assignment. Answer the question but do not go into an extended discussion. You are being examined for a *new* job, not your present one. As a matter of fact, try to phrase ALL your answers in terms of the job for which you are being examined.

Basis of Rating

Probably you will forget most of these "do's" and "don'ts" when you walk into the oral interview room. Even remembering them all will not ensure you a passing grade. Perhaps you did not have the qualifications in the first place. But remembering them will help you to put your best foot forward, without treading on the toes of the board members.

Rumor and popular opinion to the contrary notwithstanding, an oral board wants you to make the best appearance possible. They know you are under pressure – but they also want to see how you respond to it as a guide to what your reaction would be under the pressures of the job you seek. They will be influenced by the degree of poise you display, the personal traits you show and the manner in which you respond.

ABOUT THIS BOOK

This book contains tests divided into Examination Sections. Go through each test, answering every question in the margin. At the end of each test look at the answer key and check your answers. On the ones you got wrong, look at the right answer choice and learn. Do not fill in the answers first. Do not memorize the questions and answers, but understand the answer and principles involved. On your test, the questions will likely be different from the samples. Questions are changed and new ones added. If you understand these past questions you should have success with any changes that arise. Tests may consist of several types of questions. We have additional books on each subject should more study be advisable or necessary for you. Finally, the more you study, the better prepared you will be. This book is intended to be the last thing you study before you walk into the examination room. Prior study of relevant texts is also recommended. NLC publishes some of these in our Fundamental Series. Knowledge and good sense are important factors in passing your exam. Good luck also helps. So now study this Passbook, absorb the material contained within and take that knowledge into the examination. Then do your best to pass that exam.

EXAMINATION SECTION

EXAMINATION SECTION

TEST 1

DIRECTIONS: Each question or incomplete statement is followed by several suggested answers or completions. Select the one that BEST answers the question or completes the statement. *PRINT THE LETTER OF THE CORRECT ANSWER IN THE SPACE AT THE RIGHT.*

Questions 1-23

DIRECTIONS: The meters in Questions 1 through 23 are read as illustrated below.

Dial	10 reads	5
Dial	100 reads	40
Dial	1,000 reads	300
Dial	10,000 reads	8,000
Dial	100,000 reads	90,000

The reading is 98,345 cubic feet

(Assume that the maximum water consumption between consecutive meter readings was less than 100,000 cubic feet.)

1. The *correct* reading for the meter shown in the diagram above is, most nearly,
    A. 1,408 cubic feet
    B. 8,041 cubic feet
    C. 19,152 cubic feet
    D. 25,191 cubic feet

1._____

2. The *correct* reading for the meter shown in the diagram above is, most nearly,
   A. 54,545 cubic feet
   B. 65,656 cubic feet
   C. 545,454 cubic feet
   D. 656,565 cubic feet

2._____

3. The *correct* reading for the meter shown in the diagram above is, most nearly,
   A. 0 cubic feet
   B. 1 cubic foot
   C. 8 cubic feet
   D. 111,111 cubic feet

3._____

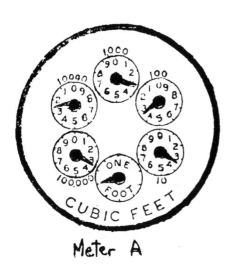
Meter A

Meter B

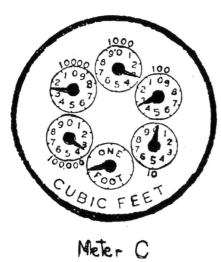
Meter C

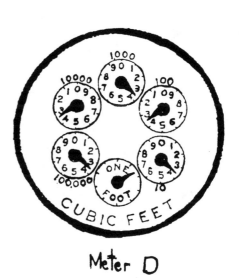
Meter D

4. In the diagram above, the meter which *most nearly* indicates a reading of 33,333 cubic feet is Meter

    A. A   B. B   C. C   D. D

4._____

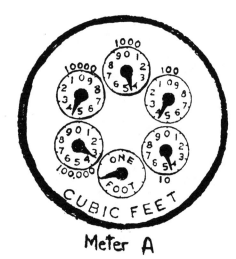
Meter A

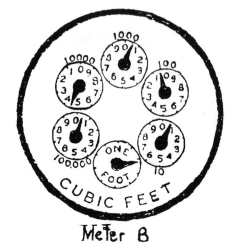
Meter B

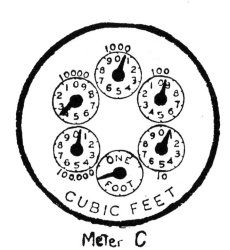
Meter C

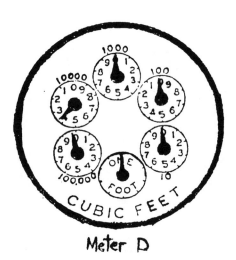
Meter D

5. In the diagram above, the meter which *most nearly* indicates a reading of four thousand cubic feet is Meter   5._____
    A. A   B. B   C. C   D. D

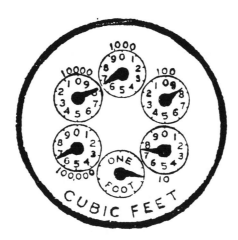

6. On the basis of the meter reading shown in the diagram above, a Water Meter Reader calculated that the water consumption between the previous reading and this reading was 9,356 cubic feet.
   Based on this information, the previous meter reading should have been, most nearly,
   A. 59,331 cubic feet
   B. 78,043 cubic feet
   C. 88,154 cubic feet
   D. 677,521 cubic feet

6._____

7. On the basis of the meter reading shown in the diagram above, a Water Meter Reader calculated that the water consumption between the previous meter reading and this reading was 1,356 cubic feet.
   Based on this information, the previous meter reading should have been, most nearly,
   A. 0 cubic feet
   B. 3,164 cubic feet
   C. 11,348 cubic feet
   D. 98,652 cubic feet

7._____

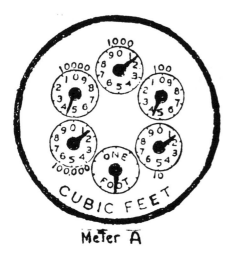
Meter A

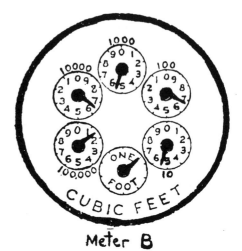
Meter B

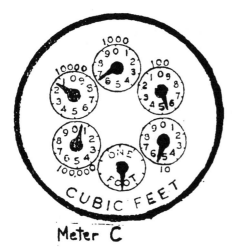
Meter C

Meter D

8. A Water Meter Reader notes that the previous reading for a certain water meter was 15,353 cubic feet. After observing the present water meter reading, he calculates that the meter indicates the water consumption between readings was most nearly 1,212 cubic feet.
The *one* of the diagrams above which most nearly shows the *present* meter reading is Meter
    A. A   B. B   C. C   D. D

8._____

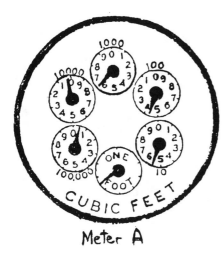
Meter A

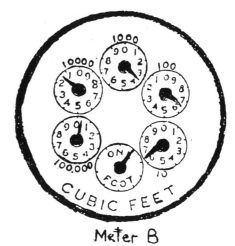
Meter B

Meter C

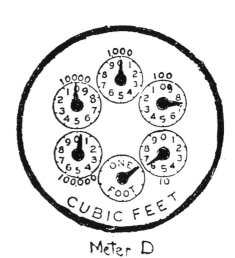
Meter D

9. A Water Meter Reader notes that the previous reading for a certain water meter was 645 cubic feet. After observing the present water meter reading, he calculates that the meter indicates the water consumption between readings was most nearly 721 cubic feet.
The *one* of the diagrams above which most nearly shows the *present* meter reading is Meter

    A. A   B. B   C. C   D. D

9._____

Previous Reading

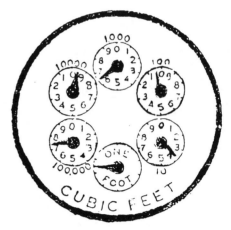

Present Reading

10. The present reading and the previous reading of a certain water meter are illustrated above. The amount of water consumed between meter readings was, most nearly,
    A. 9,824 cubic feet
    B. 17,813 cubic feet
    C. 18,814 cubic feet
    D. 19,824 cubic feet

10._____

Previous Reading

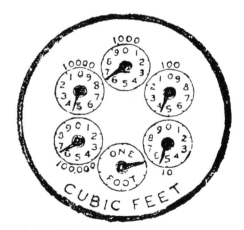

Present Reading

11. The present reading and the previous reading of a certain water meter are illustrated above. The amount of water consumed between meter readings was, most nearly,
    A. 2,025 cubic feet
    B. 3,136 cubic feet
    C. 4,686 cubic feet
    D. 6,313 cubic feet

11._____

Previous Reading   Present Reading

12. The present reading and the previous reading of a certain water meter   12._____
    are illustrated above. The amount of water consumed between meter
    readings was, most nearly,
    A. 314 cubic feet   B. 646 cubic feet
    C. 1,646 cubic feet   D. 9,354 cubic feet

Meter A   Meter B

Meter C   Meter D

13. Of the meters illustrated above, the *one* which has the *HIGHEST* reading   13._____
    is Meter
    A. A   B. B   C. C   D. D

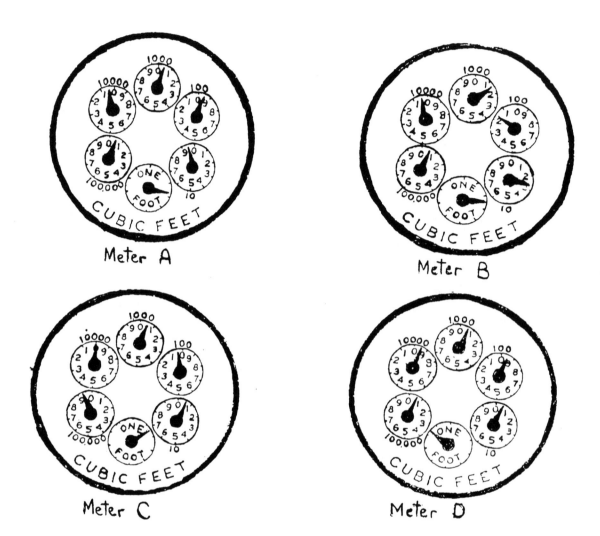

14. Of the meters illustrated above, the *one* which has the LOWEST reading is Meter

    A. A   B. B   C. C   D. D

14._____

15. If there are 7-1/2 gallons in a cubic foot of water, then the number of gallons indicated by the meter shown above is, most nearly,

    A. 149.5   B. 256   C. 3,600   D. 1117.5

15._____

16. If there are 7-1/2 gallons in a cubic foot of water, then the number of gallons indicated by the meter shown above is, most nearly,

    A. 5,154   B. 48,150   C. 6,420   D. 86

16._____

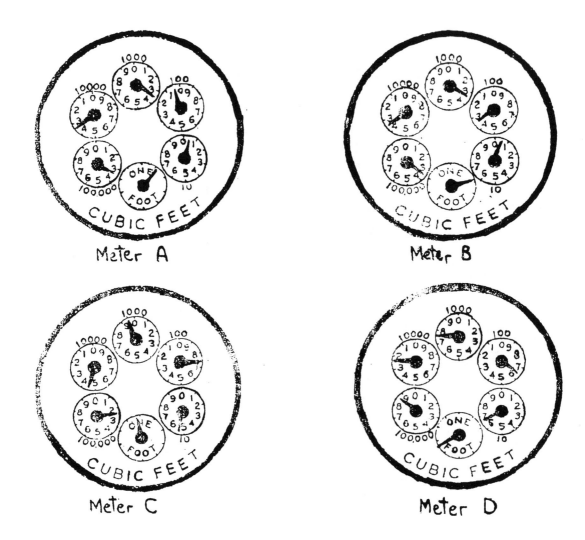

17. If there are 7-1/2 gallons in a cubic foot of water, the meter illustrated above which shows a reading equivalent to 249,750 gallons is Meter
  A. A B. B C. C D. D

17._____

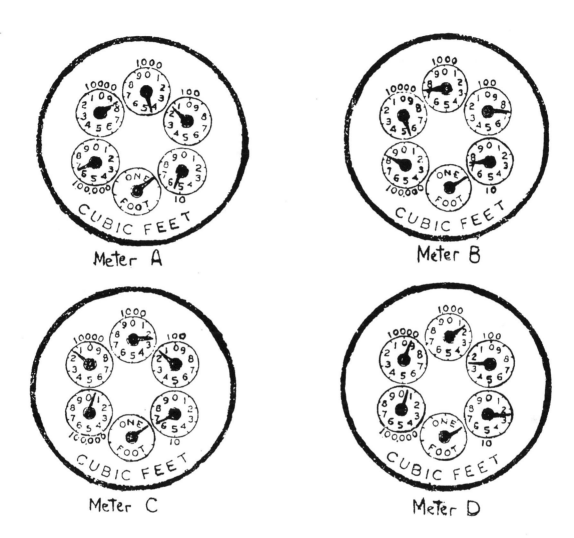

18. If there are 7-1/2 gallons in a cubic foot of water, the meter illustrated above which shows a reading equivalent to 68,415 gallons is Meter
 A. A
 B. B
 C. C
 D. D

18._____

Questions 19-20

DIRECTIONS: Answer Questions 19 and 20 on the basis of the illustration below.

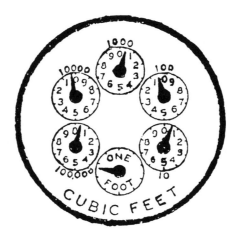

19. For each 1/4 revolution of the hand on the dial marked 100,000, the hand on the dial marked 100 revolves
    A. 25 times
    B. 250 times
    C. 2,500 times
    D. 25,000 times

    19._____

20. When the hand on the dial marked 1,000 moves from numeral 4 to numeral 9, the hand turns through an angle of
    A. 90°   B. 108°   C. 120°   D. 180°

    20._____

21. For the purpose of billing consumers, water consumption is measured by water meters. These water meters, most commonly, measure units of
    A. velocity   B. volume   C. area   D. weight

    21._____

22. When 1-5/8, 3-3/4, 6-1/3 and 9-1/2 are added, the resulting sum is
    A. 21-1/8   B. 21-1/6   C. 21-5/24   D. 21-1/4

    22._____

23. When 946-1/2 is subtracted from 1,035-1/4, the result is
    A. 87-1/4   B. 87-3/4   C. 88-1/4   D. 88-3/4

    23._____

24. When 39 is multiplied by 697, the result is
    A. 8,364   B. 26,283   C. 27,183   D. 28,003

    24._____

25. When 16.074 is divided by .045, the result is
    A. 3.6   B. 35.7   C. 357.2   D. 3,572

    25._____

Questions 26-30

DIRECTIONS: Answer Questions 26 to 30 on the basis of the information given in the table below.

Meter Readings in Cubic Feet

Date of Reading	Meter 1	Meter 2	Meter 3	Meter 4	Meter 5
Dec. 31, 2003	12,416	88,990	64,312	26,985	30,057
June 30, 2004	23,094	98,806	71,527	27,336	30,057
Dec. 31, 2004	33,011	07,723	79,292	27,848	30,618
June 30, 2005	42,907	16,915	87,208	28,286	31,247
Dec. 31, 2005	52,603	26,456	95,244	28,742	31,740

Note: The maximum readings of each of the above meters is 99,999 cubic feet. Above that reading the meters start registering from zero.
Note: Assume that the maximum water consumption between consecutive readings is less than 100,000 cubic feet.

26. The meter which showed the *LOWEST* water consumption for the period June 30, 2005 to December 31, 2005 is Meter
    A. 2   B. 3   C. 4   D. 5

    26._____

27. The amount of water consumed between June 30, 2004 and December 31, 2004 by the consumers metered by Meter 2 is
    A. 7,723 cubic feet
    B. 8,917 cubic feet
    C. 91,083 cubic feet
    D. 107,723 cubic feet

    27._____

28. The meter which showed the *GREATEST* water consumption over the time period December 31, 2003 to December 31, 2005 is Meter
    A. 1   B. 2   C. 3   D. 4

    28._____

29. The meter which showed *exactly* the same water consumption for 2005 as in 2004 is Meter
    A. 1   B. 2   C. 4   D. 5

    29._____

30. The meter which shows *exactly twice as much* water consumption in 2005 as compared to the consumption in 2004 is Meter
    A. 1   B. 3   C. 4   D. 5

    30._____

31. A certain water consumer used 5% more water in 1996 than he did in 1995. If his water consumption for 1996 was 8,375 cubic feet, the amount of water he consumed in 1995 was, most nearly,
    A. 9,014 cubic feet
    B. 8,816 cubic feet
    C. 7,976 cubic feet
    D. 6,776 cubic feet

    31._____

32. Assume that a water meter reads 40,172 cubic feet and the previous reading was 29,186 cubic feet. If the charge for water is 23 cents per 100 cubic feet or any fraction thereof, the bill for the amount of water used since the previous meter reading should be
    A. $25.07   B. $25.26   C. $25.27   D. $25.30

    32._____

33. A leaking faucet caused a loss of 216 cubic feet of water in a 30-day month.
   If there are 7-1/2 gallons in a cubic foot of water, then the *average* loss of water per hour for that month was
   A. 2-1/4 gallons
   B. 2-1/8 gallons
   C. 2 gallons
   D. 1-3/4 gallons

34. The fraction which is equal to .375 is
   A. 3/16   B. 5/32   C. 3/8   D. 5/12

35. A square backyard swimming pool, each side of which is 10 feet long, is filled to a depth of 3-1/2 feet.
   If there are 7-1/2 gallons in a cubic foot of water, the number of gallons of water in the pool is, most nearly,
   A. 46.7 gallons
   B. 100 gallons
   C. 2,625 gallons
   D. 3,500 gallons

KEY (CORRECT ANSWERS)

1. B	11. B	26. C
2. A	12. B	27. B
3. A	13. C	28. A
4. D	14. A	29. B
5. B	15. D	30. D
6. A	16. B	31. C
7. D	17. A	32. D
8. B	18. D	33. A
9. B	19. B	34. C
10. C	20. D	35. C
	21. B	
	22. C	
	23. D	
	24. C	
	25. C	

TEST 2

DIRECTIONS: Each question or incomplete statement is followed by several suggested answers or completions. Select the one that BEST answers the question or completes the statement. *PRINT THE LETTER OF THE CORRECT ANSWER IN THE SPACE AT THE RIGHT.*

1. If the water pressure at the bottom of a column of water 34 feet high is 14.7 pounds per square inch, the water pressure at the bottom of a column of water 18 feet high is, most nearly, _____ pounds per square inch.
   A. 8.0   B. 7.8   C. 7.6   D. 7.4

   1._____

2. If there are 7-1/2 gallons in a cubic foot of water and if water flows from a hose at a constant rate of 4 gallons per minute, the time it should take to *completely* fill a tank of 1,600 cubic feet capacity with water from that hose is
   A. 300 hours   B. 150 hours   C. 100 hours   D. 50 hours

   2._____

3. Each of a group of fifteen Water Meter Readers read an average of 62 water meters a day in a certain 5-day work week. A total of 5,115 meters are read by this group the following week.
   The total number of meters read in the second week as compared to the first week shows a
   A. 10% increase   B. 15% increase
   C. 20% increase   D. 5% decrease

   3._____

4. A valve which will close automatically to prevent the backflow of water in a pipe line is a _____ valve.
   A. check   B. butterfly   C. globe   D. gate

   4._____

5. The illustration to the right shows a section through a
   A. check valve
   B. butterfly valve
   C. globe valve
   D. gate valve

   5._____

6. The pipe illustrated to the right is *most commonly* known as a
   A. connector
   B. coupling
   C. sleeve
   D. nipple

   6._____

7. Brass is an alloy composed MAINLY of
   A. copper and nickel
   B. copper and zinc
   C. lead and tin
   D. lead and zinc

8. The pipe fitting illustrated to the right is known as a(n)
   A. reducing bushing
   B. return bend
   C. offset
   D. street elbow

9. The MAIN reason for "galvanizing" iron pipe is that this
   A. makes the pipe more corrosion resistant
   B. lowers the resistance of the pipe walls to liquids flowing through it
   C. makes the pipe more flexible
   D. increases the strength of the pipe

10. Of the following types of pipes, the one which is LEAST suitable for carrying hot water under pressure is
    A. copper pipe
    B. steel pipe
    C. iron pipe
    D. lead pipe

11. A pipe fitting which can be used to join the ends of two pipes, neither of which can be turned, is a
    A. union
    B. yoke
    C. Siamese connection
    D. crown weir

12. A *common* cause of water hammer in a pipe is a(n)
    A. sudden change in temperature of the pipe
    B. sudden change in water pressure in the pipe
    C. air chamber is connected to the pipe
    D. loose escutcheon is around the pipe

13. The type of wrench which is LEAST likely to be used to make up pipe joints is a(n)
    A. strap wrench
    B. Stillson wrench
    C. chain wrench
    D. Allen wrench

14. The *one* of the following types of pipe joints which is the MOST difficult to make airtight and watertight when there is pressure in the pipe is a(n)
    A. slip joint
    B. screwed joint
    C. flanged joint
    D. welded joint

15. The *one* of the following materials which is used for the manufacture of fittings but not in making pipe is
    A. cast iron
    B. malleable iron
    C. corrugated steel
    D. wrought iron

16. A bathtub faucet is installed below the flood-rim level of a bathtub. 16._____
    Of the following statements regarding this installation, the one that is
    CORRECT is: This installation is
    A. *undesirable* because it is a potential cross-connection hazard
    B. *undesirable* because the valves will be hard to manipulate by
       someone in the tub
    C. *desirable* because it prevents splashing and noise
    D. *desirable* because it causes the hot and cold water to circulate
       and mix while the tub is filling

17. The MAIN reason why standard disk-type, cold-water meters are NOT 17._____
    good for use with hot water is that the hot water will
    A. fog up the meter glass so that it cannot be read easily
    B. weaken the brass casing and cause the meter to burst
    C. cause the metal casing to expand and thus the meter will under-
       register
    D. cause the rubber and other compounds used in disks to warp or
       deteriorate

18. Compound water meters are water meters which 18._____
    A. can be used on both hot and cold water lines
    B. record both the quantity and velocity of the water flowing through
       them
    C. combine the functions of both large- and small-capacity meters
    D. electrically register the amount of water flowing through them

19. Some water meters are equipped with cast-iron bottom caps which are 19._____
    weaker than the rest of the meter. The MAIN reason for this is that these
    bottom caps
    A. make it easy to clean out the meter
    B. will break easily if the meter is tampered with
    C. will break first if ice is formed in the meter
    D. protect the meter from high electrical voltages

20. Since metering reduces water waste considerably, daily operating costs 20._____
    are similarly reduced. Less water pumped means less expense for power
    to run pumps, less chemicals for treatment, less overall overhead and
    operating expense.
    According to the above paragraph, the *one* of the following statements
    that is CORRECT is:
    A. Water is chemically treated in order to save power
    B. Water is chemically treated in order to save on overhead
    C. Metering of water means that more water must be pumped
    D. Metering of water results in less overall overhead and operating
       expenses

3 (#2)

19

21. Lack of service meters has a definite effect on water consumption. Metering of all services of a city should reduce consumption to about 50 percent of the consumption without meters. Although metering reduces water consumption, there is a tendency for consumption to increase gradually after all services are metered.
   According to the above paragraph, the *one* of the following statements that is CORRECT is:
   A. Consumption of water is cut approximately in half by metering but, once all services are metered, the consumption then increases gradually
   B. After all services are metered water consumption continues to decrease steadily
   C. Metering of all services reduces the consumption of water by much more than half
   D. Water consumption is not affected by metering of all services

22. A venturi meter operates without moving parts and hence is the simplest type of meter in use so far as its construction is concerned. It is a velocity meter and it is suitable for measuring only high rates of flow. Rates of flow below its capacity limit are not accurately measured. It is, therefore, not suitable for use in measuring the low intermittent demand of most consumers.
   According to the above paragraph, the flow in a pipe which would *most accurately* be measured by a venturi meter is
   A. an intermittent flow below the meter's capacity
   B. a steady flow below the meter's capacity
   C. a steady flow at the meter's capacity
   D. intermittent flows above or below capacity of the meter

23. A house service water-supply connection may be taken from the sprinkler water-supply connection to the public main if the diameter of the house service water-supply connection is not greater than one-half the diameter of the sprinkler water-supply connection. No shut-off valve shall be placed on the sprinkler supply line other than the main shut-off valve for the building on the street side of the house service water-supply connection. If such a connection is made and if a tap also exists for the house service water supply, the tap shall be plugged.
   According to the above paragraph, the *one* of the following statements that is CORRECT is:
   A. A sprinkler water-supply connection should be at least twice the diameter of any house service water-supply connection taken from it
   B. A shut-off valve, in addition to the main shut-off valve, is required on sprinkler supply lines on the street side of the house service water-supply connection
   C. Where a house service water supply is connected to the sprinkler water supply, and there is a tap for the house service water supply, the tap may remain in service
   D. A house service water-supply connection may be taken off each side of the main shut-off valve of the sprinkler water supply

5 (#2)

24. A Water Meter Reader discovers that a large, vicious-looking, unleashed dog is in a cellar where he is assigned to read the meter. The dog snarls whenever the Water Meter Reader approaches the cellar, but the dog's owner assures the meter reader that the dog has never bitten anyone.
Of the following, the BEST course of action for the Water Meter Reader to take is to
    A. enter the cellar and ignore the dog
    B. find a large object to carry to scare the dog
    C. try to make friends with the dog
    D. politely ask the owner to restrain the dog

24._____

25. While on an assignment to read the water meter at a certain building, a Water Meter Reader discovers evidence indicating that the water meter was illegally tampered with.
Of the following, the BEST course of action for the Water Meter Reader to take is to
    A. summon the Police Department immediately and have them check for fingerprints
    B. make a note to report this to his Department
    C. issue a summons to the person responsible for the meter without giving an explanation
    D. not report anything unless he has conclusive evidence that the water meter was indeed illegally tampered with

25._____

26. Although a water meter has a higher rating than the previous reading, a Water Meter Reader cannot tell whether the meter is in operating order because no water is running. If the only accessible faucet is badly corroded and looks very delicate, the Water Meter Reader should
    A. ask the owner to open a tap
    B. open the tap himself, but be very careful
    C. assume that the meter is working, since the new meter reading is higher
    D. loosen a pipe joint and let some water seep out, and then note whether the meter registered

26._____

27. A Water Meter Reader finds that there has been a serious fire at one of the buildings where he is assigned to read the water meter. The city has placed danger signs on the building, stating that the building is condemned.
Of the following, the BEST course of action for the Water Meter Reader to take is to
    A. enter the building and read the meter quickly before anyone interferes
    B. first put a note on the door explaining his presence, and then read the meter
    C. estimate the meter reading on the basis of past bills without entering the building
    D. note in his assignment book that the premise is condemned and not enter the building

27._____

28. At a certain business where a Water Meter Reader is assigned to read the meter, a woman refuses him entry because her husband is not home at the time.
    Of the following, the BEST course of action for the Water Meter Reader to take is to
    A. ask her to read the meter for him
    B. flash his credentials and then force his way in to read the meter
    C. summon the police and explain that she is obstructing official city business
    D. note the circumstances in his assignment book so that the Department can arrange another appointment

28._____

29. While a Water Meter Reader is reading the water meter at a small business, the owner angrily complains about the high cost of services in the city.
    Of the following, the BEST course of action for the Water Meter Reader to take is to
    A. tell the owner to be quiet and have respect for city representatives
    B. try to persuade the owner to take a more reasonable point of view
    C. listen courteously until the owner finishes talking
    D. ignore the owner's comments

29._____

30. After reading the water meter at a small business, a Water Meter Reader is approached by the owner who offers him some money if he would move several pieces of furniture.
    Of the following, the BEST course of action for the Water Meter Reader to take is to
    A. courteously refuse the job
    B. do the job for the money as long as he has enough time so that it doesn't interfere with his regular assignment
    C. do the job but refuse any payment
    D. phone his supervisor first and let him decide whether the request is reasonable

30._____

31. While a Water Meter Reader is in the field, a newspaper reporter stops him and asks for information regarding rate increases for water consumption.
    Of the following, the BEST course of action for the Water Meter Reader to take is to
    A. ignore the newspaper reporter
    B. refer him to the main office for the Department's official information
    C. tell the reporter anything he wants to know, but warn him that the information is not official
    D. give the newspaper man wrong information in order to discourage him from further questioning

31._____

32. A Water Meter Reader is assigned to read a meter in a tightly covered meter pit which has not been opened for some time. Because the meter pit is located in a chemical plant, he suspects that the accumulated air in the pit may not have enough oxygen or may be explosive.
Of the following, the FIRST safety precaution for the Water Meter Reader to take is to
    A. open the pit and test the air with a lighted match
    B. open the pit cover and allow the pit to be ventilated
    C. enter the pit slowly and sniff the air for any telltale odor
    D. lower his lighted flashlight into the pit to test for visibility

33. A Water Meter Reader is required to climb the 10' ladder shown below. Of the following, the SAFEST distance "d" that the base of the ladder should be from the wall is
    A. 1/2 foot
    B. 1-1/2 feet
    C. 2-1/2 feet
    D. 3-1/2 feet

34. Of the following, the BEST type of fire extinguisher to use on a burning oil drum is a class _____ extinguisher.
    A. A   B. B   C. C   D. D

35. A Water Meter Reader's hands become frostbitten on a cold winter day.
Of the following, the BEST first-aid treatment is to
    A. apply warm towels to his hands and give him a warm drink
    B. place his hands in cold saltwater
    C. have him rub his hands together over a warm stove
    D. place his hands in cold water and give him a warm drink

KEY (CORRECT ANSWERS)

1. B	11. A	26. A
2. D	12. B	27. D
3. A	13. D	28. D
4. A	14. A	29. C
5. C	15. B	30. A
6. D	16. A	31. B
7. B	17. D	32. B
8. D	18. C	33. C
9. A	19. C	34. B
10. D	20. D	35. A
	21. A	
	22. C	
	23. A	
	24. D	
	25. B	

EXAMINATION SECTION
TEST 1

DIRECTIONS: Each question or incomplete statement is followed by several suggested answers or completions. Select the one that BEST answers the question or completes the statement. *PRINT THE LETTER OF THE CORRECT ANSWER IN THE SPACE AT THE RIGHT.*

1. While inspecting water meters in a large office building, an inspector notices some structural beams sagging in what appears to be a dangerous manner.
   Of the following, the inspector should

   A. take no action since it is the Building Department that has jurisdiction over building structures
   B. advise the person in charge of the building to consult the Building Department
   C. notify the Police Department so that the building can be evacuated
   D. report his observation to his superior so that the Building Department can be notified

   1.____

2. Firemen sometimes find it necessary to draft salt water for use on fires. However, their departmental regulations forbid the use of salt water in any standpipe or sprinkler system.
   The MAIN reason for this prohibition is that salt water may

   A. corrode the pipes
   B. contaminate the domestic water supply
   C. cause more water damage than fresh water
   D. react chemically with some unknown substances in the building

   2.____

3. An inspector is investigating a complaint that a water meter is not operating properly. While making his examination in the basement of the building, he notices that one of the water taps is leaking.
   Of the following, the BEST course for him to follow is to

   A. recommend to his superior that another inspector be sent to the building to inspect the water taps
   B. change the washer in the tap's stem
   C. serve notice on the person in charge to correct the condition
   D. shut off the water supply to that tap

   3.____

4. An inspector who is inspecting meters finds a large dog with a menacing bark barring his way to meters in the basement of a building.
   In this situation, the BEST course of action for the inspector to follow is to

   A. try to locate the superintendent of the building
   B. make the inspection, ignoring the dog who probably will not bite
   C. leave without making the inspection and return on some other day
   D. notify the police and request that they remove the dog so that the inspection can be made

   4.____

5. Consumers are advised to turn off the water supply to their houses whenever they close the houses for any period of time.
   The MAIN reason for this practice is to prevent

   5.____

A. loss of water pressure in the event of a major fire in the area
B. build-up of excessive pressure in the pipes in the event that there is malfunctioning of the pumping system
C. occurrence of leaks during the family's absence
D. corrosion of the plumbing system during the period of disuse

6. The MAIN objection to the practice of leaving faucets open on cold nights in order to prevent freezing of water pipes is that

A. water is wasted
B. pipes will freeze even with open faucets
C. unnecessary strain is placed on the plumbing system
D. water pressure is lowered in the system

7. A permit for a tap for unmetered water will be issued only on *pre-payment* of all charges for water to be used.
The word *pre-payment*, as used above, means

A. promise of payment
B. payment in advance
C. payment as water is used
D. monthly payment

8. Upon application, the department will *endeavor* to locate a service pipe by means of an electrical indicator.
The word *endeavor*, as used above, means

A. try   B. help   C. assist   D. explore

9. It shall be unlawful for any person to operate a fire hydrant without *previous* permission from the department.
The word *previous*, as used above, means

A. written   B. oral
C. prior   D. provisional

10. All persons must *comply* with the rules and regulations.
The word *comply*, as used above, means

A. agree   B. coincide
C. work carefully   D. act in accord

11. No unauthorized person shall *tamper with* a water supply valve.
The words *tamper with*, as used above, mean

A. open   B. operate   C. alter   D. shut

12. The use of water is permitted subject to such conditions as the department may consider *reasonable*.
The word *reasonable*, as used above, means

A. necessary   B. inexpensive
C. fair   D. desirable

13. An owner must *engage* a licensed plumber.
    The word *engage,* as used above, means

    A. hire B. pay C. contact D. inform

14. The charges for a tap are usually for the *furnishing,* delivering, and installing of the tap.
    The word *furnishing*, as used above, means

    A. preparing
    C. finishing
    B. manufacturing
    D. supplying

15. The investigator attempted to *ascertain* the facts.
    As used in this sentence, the word *ascertain* means MOST NEARLY

    A. disprove
    C. go beyond
    B. find out
    D. explain

16. The speaker *commenced* the lecture with an anecdote.
    As used in this sentence, the word *commenced* means MOST NEARLY

    A. concluded
    C. enlivened
    B. illustrated
    D. started

17. The use of a hydrant may be *authorized* for construction purposes.
    The word *authorized,* as used above, means

    A. possible B. permitted C. intended D. stopped

Questions 18-20.

DIRECTIONS: Questions 18 through 20 shall be answered in accordance with the paragraph below.

A connection for commercial, purposes may be made from a metered fire or sprinkler line of 4 inches or larger in diameter, provided a meter is installed on the commercial branch line. Such connection shall be taken from the inlet side of the fire meter control valve, and the method of connection shall be subject to the approval of the department. On a 4-inch fire line, the connection shall not exceed 1 1/2 inches in diameter. On a fire line 6 inches or larger in diameter, the size of the connection shall not exceed 2 inches. Fire lines shall not be cross-connected with any system of piping within the building.

18. According to the above paragraph, a connection for commercial purposes may be made to a metered sprinkler line provided that the diameter of the sprinkler line is AT LEAST

    A. 1 1/2" B. 2" C. 4" D. 6"

19. According to the above paragraph, the connection for commercial purposes is taken from the

    A. inlet side of the main control valve
    B. outlet side of the wet connection
    C. inlet side of the fire meter control valve
    D. outlet side of the Siamese

20. According to the above paragraph, the MAXIMUM size permitted for the connection for commercial purposes depends on the 20.____

    A. location of the fire meter valve
    B. use to which the commercial line is to be put
    C. method of connection to the sprinkler line
    D. size of the sprinkler line

Questions 21-22.

DIRECTIONS: Questions 21 and 22 are to be answered in accordance with the paragraph below.

Meters shall be set or reset so that they may be easily examined and read. In all premises where the supply of water is to be fully metered, the meter shall be set within three feet of the building or vault wall at point of entry of service pipe. The service pipe between meter control valve and meter shall be kept exposed. When a building is situated back of the building line or conditions exist in a building that prevent the setting of the meter at a point of entry, meter may be set outside of the building in a proper watertight and frost-proof pit or meter box, or at other location approved by the Deputy Commissioner, Assistant to Commissioner, or the Chief Inspector.

21. According to the above paragraph, a meter should be set 21.____

    A. at a point in the building convenient to the owner
    B. within 3 feet of the building wall
    C. in back of the building
    D. where the district inspector thinks is best

22. According to the above paragraph, one of the conditions imposed when a meter is permitted to be installed outside of a building is that the meter must be installed 22.____

    A. between the service pipe and the meter control valve
    B. within 3 feet of the point of entry of the service pipe
    C. in a watertight enclosure
    D. above ground in a frost-proof box

Questions 23-26.

DIRECTIONS: Questions 23 through 26 are to be answered in accordance with the following paragraphs.

No individual or collective air conditioning system installed on any premises for a single consumer shall be permitted to waste annually more than the equivalent of a continuous flow of five gallons of city water per minute.

All individual or collective air conditioning systems installed on any premises for a single consumer using city water annually in excess of the equivalent of five gallons per minute shall be equipped with a water conserving device such as economizer, evaporative condenser, water cooling tower or other similar apparatus, which device shall not consume for make-up purposes in excess of 15% of the consumption that would normally be used without such device.

Any individual or collective group of such units installed on any premises for a single consumer with a rated capacity of 25 tons or more, or water consumption of 50 gallons or more per minute, shall be equipped, where required by the department, with a water meter to separately register the consumption of such unit or groups of units.

This rule shall also apply to all air conditioning equipment now in service.

23. The rules described in the above paragraphs apply

    A. *only* to new installations of air conditioning equipment
    B. *only* to air conditioning systems which waste more than 5 gallons of city water per minute
    C. *only* to hew installations of air conditioning equipment which waste more than 5 gallons of city water per minute
    D. to all air conditioning systems, whether existing ones or new installations

24. According to the above paragraphs, one of the acceptable methods of reducing wasting of water in an air conditioning system is by means of a

    A. cooling tower
    B. water meter
    C. check valve
    D. collective system

25. According to the above paragraphs, the department may require that an air conditioning system have a separate water meter when the system

    A. wastes more than 5 gallons of city water per minute
    B. uses more than 15% make-up water
    C. is equipped with an economizer
    D. has a rated capacity of 25 tons or more

26. According to the above paragraphs, the MAXIMUM quantity of make-up water permitted where an air conditioning system uses 50 gallons of water per minute is _____ gal./min.

    A. 7
    B. 7 1/2
    C. 8
    D. 8 1/2

Questions 27-28.

DIRECTIONS: Questions 27 and 28 are to be answered in accordance with the paragraph below.

Where flushometers, suction tanks, other fixtures or piping are equipped with quick closing valves and are supplied by direct street pressure in excess of 70 pounds, an air chamber of an approved type shall be installed within two feet of the house control valve or meter in the service near the point of entry. Where water hammer conditions exist in any installation, regardless of the pressure obtaining, an air chamber of an approved type shall be installed where and as directed by the Chief Inspector or Engineer.

27. According to the above paragraph, air chambers are required when or wherever

    A. there are flushometers
    B. piping is supplied at a direct street pressure in excess of 70 lbs. per square inch
    C. a quick closing valve is used
    D. water hammer can occur in any piping

28. According to the above paragraph, air chambers should be installed

   A. within two feet of the house control valve or meter
   B. in a water system regardless of operating pressure
   C. on the fixture side of the quick closing valve
   D. on the suction side of the service meter

Questions 29-32.

DIRECTIONS: Questions 29 through 32, inclusive, refer to the paragraphs, tables, and building floor plans shown below.

The annual frontage rents on premises wholly or partly unmetered shall be as follows:

Front Width of Building	One Story Height	Front Width of Building	One Story Height
16 ft. and under	$ 6.00	Over 22 1/2 ft. -25 ft.	$12.00
Over 16 ft. -18 ft.	7.50	Over 25 ft. -20 ft.	15.00
Over 18 ft. -20 ft.	9.00	Over 30 ft. -37 1/2 ft.	18.00
Over 20 ft. -22 1/2 ft.	10.50	Over 37 1/2 ft. -50 ft.	21.00

For each additional story, $1.50 per annum shall be added; and for each additional ten (10) feet or part thereof above fifty feet in front width of building, $3.00 shall be added.

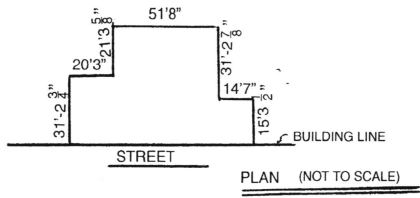

PLAN (NOT TO SCALE)

29. The front width of this building is

   A. 85'11"   B. 86'0"   C. 86'1"   D. 86'2"

30. The MAXIMUM depth of the above building is

   A. 51'5 3/4"   B. 52'5"   C. 52'6 3/8"   D. 66'7 3/8"

31. If the above building is only one story high, the frontage rent is

   A. $30.00   B. $31.50   C. $33.00   D. $34.50

32. If the above building is three stories high, the frontage rent is

   A. $31.50   B. $33.00   C. $34.50   D. $36.00

33. Of the following materials, the one which is NOT used in the city for supplying domestic water in a plumbing system is   33.____

   A. red brass
   B. yellow brass
   C. plastic
   D. galvanized cast iron

34. A simple pressure gauge installed on a water line is USUALLY used to _____ water pressure.   34.____

   A. relieve excessive
   B. control the
   C. measure the
   D. decrease the

35. A *standpipe system* is generally used to supply water to the   35.____

   A. domestic water system
   B. wet sprinkler system
   C. fire hose
   D. house tank

KEY (CORRECT ANSWERS)

1.	D	16.	D
2.	B	17.	B
3.	C	18.	C
4.	A	19.	C
5.	C	20.	D
6.	A	21.	B
7.	B	22.	C
8.	A	23.	D
9.	C	24.	A
10.	D	25.	D
11.	C	26.	B
12.	C	27.	D
13.	A	28.	A
14.	D	29.	B
15.	B	30.	C

31. C
32. D
33. C
34. C
35. C

TEST 2

DIRECTIONS: Each question or incomplete statement is followed by several suggested answers or completions. Select the one that BEST answers the question or completes the statement. *PRINT THE LETTER OF THE CORRECT ANSWER IN THE SPACE AT THE RIGHT.*

Questions 1-4.

DIRECTIONS: Questions 1 through 4, inclusive, refer to the sketches of the floor plan of 3 buildings shown below.

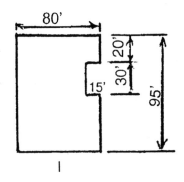

I

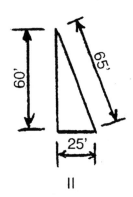

II

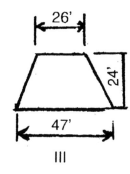

III

Sketches not to scale

1. The area in square feet of each floor of building #I is MOST NEARLY   1._____
   A. 7150   B. 7600   C. 8050   D. 8500

2. The area in square feet of each floor of building #II is MOST NEARLY   2._____
   A. 750   B. 817   C. 1500   D. 1625

3. The area in square feet of each floor of building #III is MOST NEARLY   3._____
   A. 504   B. 876   C. 1460   D. 1756

4. The area of building #I is MOST NEARLY _____ times that of building #III.   4._____
   A. 5   B. 6   C. 7   D. 8

5. The plumbing term *furred-in* generally means that the plumbing pipes are   5.____

    A. hidden   B. exposed
    C. insulated   D. made watertight

Questions 6-9.

DIRECTIONS: Questions 6 through 9, inclusive, refer to the diagram of the dials of a water meter shown below.

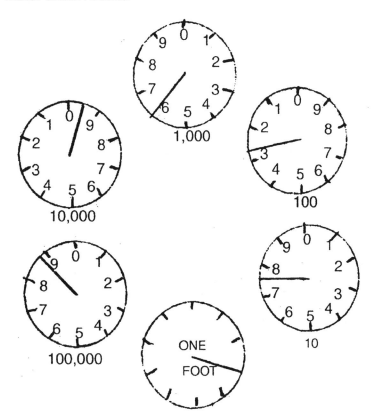

6. The CORRECT reading of the meter, in cubic feet, is   6.____

    A. 72698   B. 89627   C. 90637   D. 80637

7. For each complete revolution of the hand on the dial marked 10,000, the hand on the dial   7.____
   marked 10 revolves _____ times.

    A. 3   B. 20   C. 300   D. 1,000

8. The statement MOST NEARLY CORRECT is that the hands on _____ rotate in a   8.____
   _____ direction.

    A. all the dials; clockwise
    B. all the dials; counterclockwise
    C. the dials marked 10, 1,000, and 100,000; clockwise
    D. the dials marked 10, 1,000, and 100,000; counterclockwise

9. If the hand on the 1000 dial was exactly on the number 7, and then moved to the number 8, the hand on the 100 dial would move

   A. one space clockwise
   B. completely around the dial and stop in the same place it was originally
   C. one space counterclockwise
   D. one or more spaces, depending on the water flow

9.____

10. The MAIN purpose of a house roof tank for plumbing fixtures in a building is to

    A. conserve usage of water
    B. provide a storage place when the water is not in demand
    C. insure necessary water pressure at the plumbing fixtures
    D. provide a means of chemically treating the water

10.____

11. A short piece of straight 1/2" diameter pipe 2" long and having male threads at both ends is USUALLY called a

    A. coupling   B. union   C. nipple   D. stud

11.____

12. A hypochlorite solution is USUALLY used for

    A. disinfecting water tanks
    B. soldering
    C. preventing rust formation in pipes
    D. cleaning water meters

12.____

13. The size of a water meter is USUALLY governed by the

    A. diameter of the service pipe
    B. diameter of the tap
    C. available space where installed
    D. pressure in the main

13.____

14. An automatic water regulating valve is a valve that is

    A. free flowing   B. one way
    C. self-regulating   D. a control valve

14.____

15. The MINIMUM diameter, in inches, of water supply branches made of ferrous material, connected to fixtures other than those connected to flush valves is

    A. 3/8"   B. 1/2"   C. 5/8"   D. 3/4"

15.____

16. The type of water meter that operates without moving parts is GENERALLY known as a _____ meter.

    A. compound   B. venturi   C. turbine   D. disc

16.____

17. A water service pipe is USUALLY laid in a straight line at right angles to the street main in order to

    A. increase frictional losses
    B. make rodding easier
    C. shorten the run of pipe
    D. reduce the amount of excavation

17.____

18. The size of a water service pipe for commercial and industrial use is USUALLY determined on the basis of the

   A. building floor area
   B. water pressure
   C. number of floors in a building
   D. water demand load

19. The MINIMUM size of service pipe permitted for commercial and industrial use is

   A. 3/4"   B. 1"   C. 1 1/4"   D. 1 1/2"

20. The size of a corporation cock should be

   A. one size smaller than the size of service pipe
   B. one size larger than the size of service pipe
   C. equal to the size of service pipe
   D. not greater than 3/4"

21. A *wet connection* is made when the water in the main is

   A. shut off
   B. under pressure
   C. by-passed
   D. leaking

22. A corporation cock is used MAINLY for

   A. shutting off the water
   B. tap connections
   C. regulating the flow
   D. wet connections

23. The size of the hole permitted in the water main for a tap connection depends upon the

   A. size of the main
   B. pressure in the main
   C. pipe material of the main
   D. spacing of the taps

24. A water service pipe is defined as that portion of the water pipe extending from the public main to the

   A. curb valve and box
   B. furthest fixture
   C. building line
   D. main house control valve

25. The type of water meter, 3" or larger, that is USUALLY used where there is a fluctuating flow of water or a pressure feed water system is called a _____ meter.

   A. displacement
   B. current
   C. compound
   D. fire-service

26. A water meter is a device that is used to measure the water

   A. pressure   B. velocity   C. consumed   D. hardness

27. A pressure of 25 psi in the street main may be sufficient to supply water to a building that is NOT more than _____ feet high.

   A. 40   B. 60   C. 80   D. 100

28. The MINIMUM distance that a vacuum breaker should be set, above the floor level rim of a fixture, is

    A. 1" B. 2" C. 3" D. 4"

29. The one of the following types of buildings which does NOT require the installation of a water meter is a

    A. public library
    B. hotel
    C. factory
    D. canning plant

30. The city is NOT required to maintain a minimum water pressure in a premise other than that required to deliver water to the

    A. top floor fixture
    B. roof tank
    C. standpipe system (gravity)
    D. basement

31. After a tap has been inserted in a water main and the service pipe installed, the type of backfill around and one foot over the main and service should be

    A. clean earth
    B. gravel
    C. asphalt concrete
    D. tanbark

32. According to the city code, water supply lines to hot water boilers, steam boilers, or similar equipment MUST be equipped with a

    A. vacuum breaker
    B. check valve
    C. pressure reducing valve
    D. compound gauge

33. The one of the following chemicals which is used to soften water is

    A. calcium carbonate
    B. slaked lime
    C. magnesium sulphate
    D. calcium chloride

34. A sounding rod is used to

    A. locate leaks in buried water pipes
    B. locate the trouble in a noisy meter
    C. determine the cause of pipe vibration
    D. locate water hammer in a pipe line

35. The purpose of a float-controlled valve used in a water-closet flush tank is to maintain a

    A. continuous water supply to the tank
    B. constant water level in the tank
    C. back pressure in the water line
    D. quiet water feed

KEY (CORRECT ANSWERS)

1.	A	16.	B
2.	A	17.	B
3.	B	18.	D
4.	D	19.	B
5.	A	20.	A
6.	B	21.	B
7.	D	22.	D
8.	C	23.	A
9.	B	24.	D
10.	C	25.	C
11.	C	26.	C
12.	A	27.	A
13.	B	28.	D
14.	C	29.	A
15.	B	30.	D

31. A
32. B
33. B
34. A
35. B

EXAMINATION SECTION
TEST 1

DIRECTIONS: Each question or incomplete statement is followed by several suggested answers or completions. Select the one that BEST answers the question or completes the statement. *PRINT THE LETTER OF THE CORRECT ANSWER IN THE SPACE AT THE RIGHT.*

Questions 1-2.

DIRECTIONS: Questions 1 and 2 are to be answered on the basis of the passage below.

When summers are hot and dry, much water will be used for watering lawns. Domestic use will be further increased by more bathing, while public use will be affected by much street sprinkling and use in parks and recreation fields for watering grass and for ornamental fountains. Variations in the weather may cause variations in water consumption. A succession of showers in the summer could significantly reduce water consumption. High temperatures may also lead to high water use for air-conditioning purposes. On the other hand, in cold weather, water may be wasted at the faucets to prevent freezing of pipes, thereby greatly increasing consumption.

1. According to the above passage, water consumption

    A. will not be affected by the weather to any appreciable extent
    B. will always increase in the warm weather and decrease in cold weather
    C. will increase in cold weather and decrease in warm weather
    D. may increase because of high or low temperatures

2. The MAIN subject of the above passage is:

    A. Climatic conditions affecting water consumption
    B. Water consumption in arid regions
    C. Conservation of water
    D. Weather variations

Questions 3-4.

DIRECTIONS: Questions 3 and 4 are to be answered on the basis of the passage below.

The efficiency of the water works management will affect consumption by decreasing loss and waste. Leaks in the water mains and services and unauthorized use of water can be kept to a minimum by surveys. A water supply that is both safe and attractive in quality will be used to a greater extent than one of poor quality. In this connection, it should be recognized that improvement of the quality of water supply will probably be followed by an increase in consumption. Increasing the pressure will have a similar effect. Changing the rates charged for water will also affect consumption. A study found that consumption decreases about five percent for each ten percent increase in water rates. Similarly, water consumption increases when the water rates are decreasing.

3. According to the above passage, an increase in the quality of water would MOST likely   3.____

   A. cause an increase in water consumption
   B. decrease water consumption by about 10%
   C. cause a decrease in water consumption
   D. have no effect on water consumption

4. According to the above passage, a ten percent decrease in water rates would MOST   4.____
   likely result in a _____ percent _____ in the water consumption.

   A. five; decrease   B. five; increase
   C. ten; decrease   D. ten; increase

Questions 5-6.

DIRECTIONS: Questions 5 and 6 are to be answered on the basis of the passage below.

   While the average domestic use of water may be expected to be about 35 gallons per person daily, wide variations are found. These are largely dependent upon the economic status of the consumers and will differ greatly in various sections of the city. In the high value residential districts of a city or in a suburban community of similar type population, the water consumption per person will be high. In apartment houses, which may be considered as representing the maximum domestic demand to be expected, the average consumption should be about 60 gallons per person. In an area of high value single residences, even higher consumption may be expected, since to the ordinary domestic demand there will be added amount for watering lawns. The slum districts of large cities will show a consumption per person of about 20 gallons daily. The lowest figures of all will be found in low value districts, where sewerage is not available and where perhaps a single faucet serves one or several households.

5. According to the above passage, domestic water consumption per person   5.____

   A. would probably be lowest for persons in an area of high value single residences
   B. would probably be lowest for persons in an apartment house
   C. would probably be lowest for persons in a slum area
   D. does not depend at all upon area or income

6. According to the above passage, the water consumption in apartment houses as com-   6.____
   pared to slum houses is about _____ times as much.

   A. 1 1/2   B. 2   C. 2 1/2   D. 3

Questions 7-8.

DIRECTIONS: Questions 7 and 8 are to be answered on the basis of the passage below.

   One of the greatest hazards to an industrial plant is fire. Consequently, a rigid system should be set up for periodic inspection of all types of fire protective equipment. Such inspections should include water tanks, sprinkler systems, standpipes, hose, fire plugs, extinguishers, and all other equipment used for fire protection. The schedule of inspections should be closely followed and an ACCURATE record kept of each piece of equipment inspected and tested.

Along with this scheduled inspection, a careful survey should be made of new equipment needed. Recommendations should be made for replacement of defective and obsolete equipment, as well as the purchase of any additional equipment. As new processes and products are added to the manufacturing system, new fire hazards may be introduced that require individual treatment and possible special extinguishing devices. Plant inspection personnel should be sure to follow through.

Surveys should also include all means of egress from the building. Exits, stairs, fire towers, fire escapes, halls, fire alarm systems, emergency lighting systems, and places seldom used should be thoroughly inspected to determine their adequacy and readiness for emergency use.

7. Of the following titles, the one that BEST fits the above passage is:

    A. NEW, USED, AND OLD FIRE PROTECTION EQUIPMENT
    B. MAINTENANCE OF FIRE PROTECTION EQUIPMENT
    C. INSPECTION OF FIRE PROTECTION EQUIPMENT
    D. OVERHAUL OF WORN OUT FIRE FIGHTING EQUIPMENT

8. As used in the above passage, the word ACCURATE means

    A. exact
    B. approximate
    C. close
    D. vague

9. In talking with a homeowner, an inspector should always be *polite*.
As used in the above statement, the word *polite* means

    A. cold   B. courteous   C. aggressive   D. modest

10. In talking with a homeowner, an inspector should not discuss *trivial* matters.
As used in the above statement, the word *trivial* means

    A. related
    B. essential
    C. significant
    D. unimportant

11. The one of the following words that is SIMILAR in meaning to *revise* is

    A. edit
    B. confuse
    C. complicate
    D. dismiss

12. The one of the following words that is SIMILAR in meaning to *abandon* is

    A. quit   B. use   C. remain   D. discourage

13. The one of the following words that is SIMILAR in meaning to *adjacent* is

    A. far   B. detached   C. bordering   D. distant

14. The one of the following words that is SIMILAR in meaning to *coarse* is

    A. fine   B. smooth   C. rough   D. slick

15. The one of the following words that is SIMILAR in meaning to *orifice* is

    A. chamber   B. enclosure   C. opening   D. device

16. The one of the following words that has the OPPOSITE meaning of *partition* is 16.____

    A. division B. connection
    C. barrier   D. compartment

17. The one of the following words that has the OPPOSITE meaning of *obvious* is 17.____

    A. concealed B. known C. clear D. apparent

18. The one of the following words that has the OPPOSITE meaning of *assist* is 18.____

    A. hinder B. offer C. demand D. aid

19. The one of the following words that has the OPPOSITE meaning of *obsolete* is 19.____

    A. neglected B. traditional
    C. rare   D. new

20. The one of the following words that has the OPPOSITE meaning of *stagnant* is 20.____

    A. murky B. active C. calm D. dirty

21. The number of gallons of water contained in a cylindrical swimming pool 8 feet in diameter and filled to a depth of 3 feet 6 inches is MOST NEARLY (assume 7.5 gallons = 1 cubic foot) 21.____

    A. 30 B. 225 C. 1695 D. 3000

22. An inspector observes a meter reading of 02321 cu.ft. on a straight reading type of register. The previous reading on that meter for that location was 99332. 22.____
    The amount of water used between readings, assuming no backflow through the meter, was MOST NEARLY _____ cu.ft.

    A. -97511 B. 2489 C. 12489 D. 97511

Questions 23-24.

DIRECTIONS: Questions 23 and 24 are to be answered on the basis of the diagram of the dials of water meter shown below.

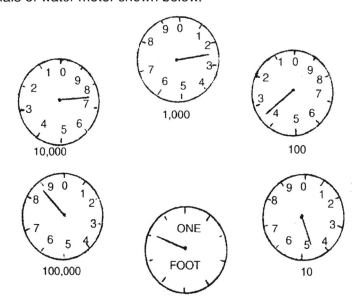

23. The CORRECT water meter reading, in cubic feet, is 23._____

    A. 43278   B. 54389   C. 87234   D. 98345

24. For each half revolution of the hand on the 10,000 dial, the hand on the indicator marked 10 will revolve _____ revolutions. 24._____

    A. 50   B. 500   C. 5,000   D. 50,000

25. If a 100-foot steel pipe expands 5/8 inch when the temperature rises 20° F, then the expansion of a steel pipe 40 feet long when the temperature rises 60° F is MOST NEARLY 25._____

    A. 1/2"   B. 5/8"   C. 3/4"   D. 7/8"

KEY (CORRECT ANSWERS)

1. D
2. A
3. A
4. B
5. C

6. D
7. C
8. A
9. B
10. D

11. A
12. A
13. C
14. C
15. C

16. B
17. A
18. A
19. D
20. B

21. C
22. B
23. C
24. B
25. C

TEST 2

DIRECTIONS: Each question or incomplete statement is followed by several suggested answers or completions. Select the one that BEST answers the question or completes the statement. *PRINT THE LETTER OF THE CORRECT ANSWER IN THE SPACE AT THE RIGHT.*

1.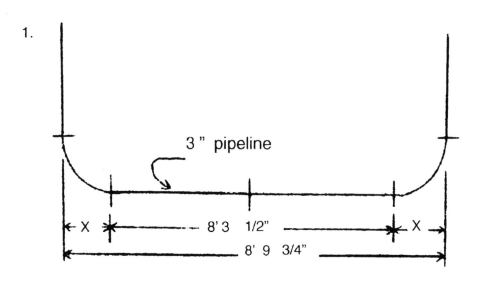

   In the above sketch of a 3" pipeline, the distance X is MOST NEARLY _____ inches.

   A. 3 1/8   B. 3 1/4   C. 3 1/2   D. 3 5/8

2. The fraction 9/64 is MOST NEARLY equal to

   A. .1375   B. .1406   C. .1462   D. .1489

3. The sum of the following dimensions is 1'2 3/6", 1'5 1/2", and 1'4 5/8" is

   A. 3'11 15/16"   B. 4'5/16"
   C. 4'11/16"   D. 4'1 5/8"

4. The scale on a plumbing drawing is 1/8" = 1 foot. A horizontal line measuring 3 5/16" on the drawing would represent a length of _____ feet.

   A. 24.9   B. 26.5   C. 28.3   D. 30.2

5. Assume that a water meter reads 50,631 cubic feet and the previous reading was 39,842 cubic feet.
   If the charge for water is 230 per 100 cubic feet or any fraction thereof, the bill for the amount of water used since the previous meter reading will be MOST NEARLY

   A. $24.22   B. $24.38   C. $24.84   D. $24.95

6. At a certain premises, the water consumption was 4 percent higher in 2005 than it was in 2004.
   If the water consumption for 2005 was 9740 cubic feet, then the water consumption for 2004 was MOST NEARLY _____ cubic feet.

   A. 9320   B. 9350   C. 9365   D. 9390

7. A pump delivers water at a constant rate of 40 gallons per minute. If there are 7.5 gallons to a cubic foot of water, the time it will take to fill a tank 6 ft. x 5 ft. x 4 ft. is MOST NEARLY _____ minutes.

   A. 15 B. 22.5 C. 28.5 D. 30

8. The total weight, in pounds, of three lengths of 3" cast iron pipe 7'6" long, weighing 14.5 pounds per foot, and four lengths of 4" cast iron pipe each 5'0" long, weighing 13.0 pounds per foot, is MOST NEARLY

   A. 540 B. 585 C. 600 D. 665

9. The water pressure at the bottom of a column of water 34 feet high is 14.7 lbs./sq.in. The water pressure, in lbs./sq.in., at the bottom of a column of water 12 feet high is MOST NEARLY

   A. 3 B. 5 C. 7 D. 9

10. The number of cubic yards of earth that would be removed when digging a trench 8 ft. wide x 9 ft. deep x 63 ft. long is

    A. 56 B. 168 C. 314 D. 504

11. If a newspaper man asks an inspector for facts about his job activities, the BEST of the following courses of action for the inspector to take is to

    A. be as evasive as possible
    B. refer him to the main office of the responsible department
    C. tell him everything off the record
    D. ignore the reporter altogether

12. Before entering a tightly covered water meter pit, it is MOST advisable for an inspector to FIRST

    A. remove pit cover and test for gas in the pit with a lighted match
    B. check pit cover joints with soap solution for seepage of gas and then remove pit cover
    C. remove pit cover and allow the pit to be ventilated
    D. remove pit cover and enter pit using a handkerchief as a mask to filter out any harmful gases

13. While a building owner is escorting an inspector to the cellar of the building, the building owner slips on the cellar stairs and falls and breaks his leg.
    Of the following types of first aid procedures, the one that is BEST for the inspector to take in this case is to

    A. move the victim to a warm place
    B. place the victim's leg in cold water to minimize swelling
    C. keep the victim still and try to keep him warm
    D. give the victim a stimulant to drink

14. An inspector finds that the sidewalk cellar door is open at a premises in which he is supposed to read the water meter.
    Of the following, the BEST course of action for him to take is to

    A. enter the cellar and read the meter before anyone interferes
    B. obtain authorization from a responsible person at the premises before entering the cellar
    C. make some deliberate noise, by banging on the door, to determine if an unrestrained dog is on the premises and, if not, enter the cellar
    D. make an estimate of the meter reading to save the time and effort of searching through the cellar

15. While reading water meters at a premise, an inspector is confronted by the owner who asks him to clean out the clogged drain of a kitchen sink.
    Of the following, the BEST course of action for the inspector to take is to

    A. comply with the request for a small fee, if it does not interfere with the day's assignment
    B. attempt the job for non-monetary compensation
    C. recommend the Roto-Rooter man
    D. politely refuse to comply with the request

16. The rules and regulations governing and restricting the use and supply of water allow authorized meter repair companies, with a meter repair permit, to make repairs on the premises of

    A. hot water meters, regardless of size but not cold water meters
    B. cold water meters, regardless of size, and hot water meters larger than three inches in size
    C. all meters less than three inches in size, hot or cold water
    D. only cold water meters, three inches in size and larger

17. According to the rules and regulations governing and restricting the use and supply of water, all water meter valves should be standard _____ valves.

    A. gate   B. globe   C. needle   D. angle

18. According to the rules and regulations governing and restricting the use and supply of water, the water which must be metered in the construction of an eight-story apartment building is

    A. only the water used in building the seventh and eighth stories
    B. all the water used in the construction of that building
    C. all the water used after the basement is constructed
    D. none at all, since the building is not a commercial establishment

19. According to the rules and regulations governing and restricting the use and supply of water, a meter pit must have an air vent if the meter pit contains a(n)

    A. meter by-pass   B. sewer trap
    C. airtight metal door   D. meter outlet valve

20. According to the rules and regulations governing and restricting the use and supply of water, on a 1" meter setting, the check valve shall be placed between the

    A. front wall and the service valve
    B. service valve and the meter
    C. meter and the test tee
    D. test tee and the outlet valve

21. The plumbing connection illustrated at the right is a(n)

    A. *correct* installation according to the building code
    B. *incorrect* installation because it is illegal for a drain to empty into a stack
    C. *incorrect* installation because each lavatory should enter into a separate stack
    D. *incorrect* installation because the two wastes should enter the stack at a higher elevation with respect to the trap

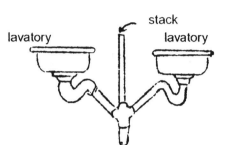

22.

The plumbing connection illustrated on the previous page is a(n)

    A. *correct* installation according to the building code
    B. *incorrect* installation because the check valve should be located on the hot water line
    C. *incorrect* installation because the gate valves should be eliminated
    D. *incorrect* installation because the hot water storage tank should be vented to the atmosphere

23.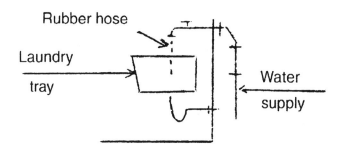

The connection illustrated above is a(n)

- A. *correct* installation according to the building code
- B. *incorrect* installation because the faucets should be located below the rim to prevent splashing
- C. *incorrect* installation because the hanging hose forms a potential cross connection
- D. *incorrect* installation because the hot water can enter the cold water pipe

24. Of the following, the indication that would cause the MOST suspicion that a water meter may have been illegally tampered with is

- A. a seal wire broken by corrosion
- B. fresh wrench marks on a meter outlet valve
- C. a new coat of paint on the water meter and surrounding pipes
- D. missing glass on the meter register

25. An inspector finds that water is being wasted at a commercial establishment because of a faulty regulator valve on the air conditioner at the premise.
Of the following, the BEST course of action for him to take is to

- A. issue a summons to the owner of the premise
- B. issue a notice of non-compliance to the owner of the premise
- C. immediately notify a licensed plumber so that he will make the necessary repair
- D. ignore the situation since all air conditioners use well water

KEY (CORRECT ANSWERS)

1. A
2. B
3. B
4. B
5. C

6. C
7. B
8. B
9. B
10. B

11. B
12. C
13. C
14. B
15. D

16. D
17. A
18. B
19. B
20. D

21. D
22. A
23. C
24. D
25. B

EXAMINATION SECTION
TEST 1

DIRECTIONS: Each question or incomplete statement is followed by several suggested answers or completions. Select the one that BEST answers the question or completes the statement. *PRINT THE LETTER OF THE CORRECT ANSWER IN THE SPACE AT THE RIGHT.*

1. On December 15, you see a consumer watering his lawn by means of a hose. Of the following, *you should*

    A. check to see whether connection is to an inside coupling
    B. make a mental note that his water charges should be higher the next time his meter is read
    C. tell him he is violating the law and should stop
    D. report this act to your supervisor at the end of the month

    1.____

2. You notice a leak in a plumbing fixture while taking a meter reading. The BEST reason for instructing the consumer to repair this defect is to

    A. create good will
    B. decrease the consumer's water charges
    C. prevent water pollution
    D. prevent water waste

    2.____

3. You notice that a water meter is not registering even though the water is turned on. You *should*

    A. inform you supervisor
    B. install a new meter yourself
    C. repair the meter yourself
    D. shut off the water

    3.____

4. You find the seal broken on a meter you are reading. You *should*

    A. order the consumer to reseal the meter at once
    B. report the fact to your supervisor
    C. reseal the meter yourself and say nothing, hoping you can catch the culprit
    D. test the meter yourself, making the consumer bear the cost

    4.____

5. A consumer uses abusive language in objecting to his water charges. You *should*

    A. agree with him simply to quiet him but determine to do nothing for such a person
    B. call a policeman and have him arrested
    C. listen quietly until he finishes and then explain what can be done according to regulations to correct the trouble
    D. tell him you don't have to listen to such talk and leave

    5.____

6. The meter system, as compared to the flat rate system of water charges based on frontage, is:

    A. *advantageous* because it eliminates unauthorized use of water
    B. *not advantageous* because of cost of meter maintenance

    6.____

C. *advantageous* because it tends to reduce water waste
D. *not advantageous* because of expense of installation

7. Of the following, a meter's *most important* advantage is that it

   A. can be easily discarded it it doesn't work
   B. is easy to keep in repair
   C. is inexpensive to install
   D. offers a fair basis for billing consumer

8. Regulations state that street showers shall be operated only when the outdoor temperature is 80°F or higher. The BEST reason for this is the

   A. aid to street sanitation
   B. lack of necessary department help
   C. prevention of colds
   D. prevention of water waste

9. The size and number of taps or connections for a water supply line to a building *usually* depends on the

   A. total floor area
   B. total number of people to occupy the building
   C. total number of water fixtures
   D. zone in which the building is located

10. The objection to a siphonable plumbing- fixture is that it

    A. does not register accurately on water meters
    B. is a health hazard
    C. is expensive
    D. wastes water

Questions 11-15.

DIRECTIONS: Questions 11 to 15 are based on the meters shown on the following page.

11. The *correct* reading for Meter A is:

    A. 3,888   B. 92,777   C. 203,888   D. 292,777

12. The *correct* reading for Meter B is:

    A. 8,999   B. 88,990   C. 99,000   D. 188,990

13. The *correct* reading for Meter C is:

    A. 9,826   B. 110,937   C. 5,009,826   D. 6,110,937

14. The *correct* reading for Meter D is:

    A. 5,609   B. 945,989   C. 994,598   D. 9,945,989

3 (#1)

15. Assume that in Meter A the correct reading is 4,331 cubic feet. The last previous reading was 84,622 cubic feet. Consumption, in cubic feet, between the two readings has been   15.____

    A. 4,331   B. 19,709   C. 80,291   D. 88,953

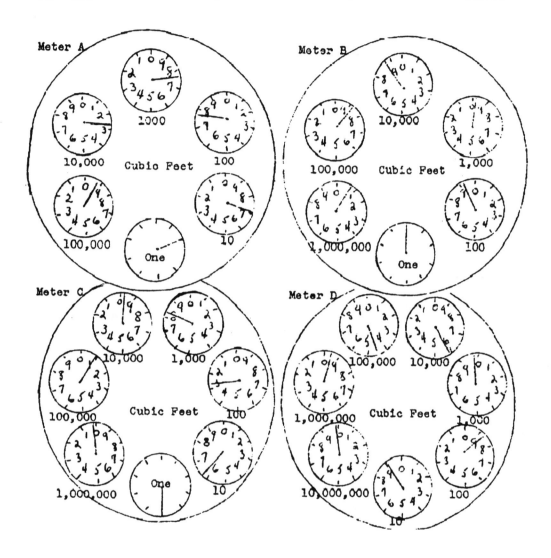

Questions 16-20.

DIRECTIONS: Answer questions 16 to 20 *only* on the basis of the information contained in the following statement of water charges based on frontage.

The annual frontage rents on premises wholly or partly un-metered shall be as follows:

FRONT WIDTH OF BUILDING	ONE-STORY
16 feet and under	$6.00
Over 16 feet to 18 feet	7.00
Over 18 feet to 20 feet	9.00
Over 20 feet to 22 1/2 feet	10.50
Over 22 1/2 feet to 25 feet	12.00
Over 25 feet to 30 feet	15.00
Over 30 feet to 37 1/2 feet	18.00
Over 37 1/2 feet to 50 feet	21.00

For each additional story} $1.50 per annum shall be added, and) for eaoh additional ten (10) feet or part thereof above fifty (50) feet in front width of building} $3.00 shall be added.

The apportionment is on the basis that but one family is to occupy premises and., for each additional family or apartment, $1.50 per year shall be charged.

Baths in excess of one (1) to each house shall be charged at the rate of $4.50 each per annum.

16. The annual frontage rent on an unmetered one-story building. 18 1/2 feet wide, occupied by two families, each having one bath, is

    A. $9.00
    B. $15.00
    C. $21.00
    D. None of the above

17. The annual frontage rent on an unmetered two-story building, 33 feet wide, occupied by four families, each having one bath, is

    A. $15.00
    B. $36.00
    C. $43.50
    D. None of the above

18. The annual frontage rent on a four-story building, 51 feet wide, occupied by eight families, each two families sharing one bath, is

    A. $49.50
    B. $52.50
    C. $66.00
    D. None of the above

19. The annual frontage rent on a three-story building, 72 feet wide, occupied by six families, each having two baths, is

    A. $60.00
    B. $84.00
    C. $90.00
    D. None of the above

20. The annual frontage rent for a one-story building, 12 feet wide, occupied by one family, having one bath, is

    A. $3.00
    B. $7.50
    C. $12.00
    D. None of the above

Questions 21-25.

DIRECTIONS: Answer questions 21 to 25 *only* on the basis of the information contained in the following paragraph:

Meter rates at present are 15 cents per 100 cubic feet. The meter rates remained the same from 1950 to the end of 1991. Beginning January 1, 1992, these rates were increased a flat 50 per cent.

21. The charge for 98,300 cubic feet of water at present   21._____

    A. is $98.30
    B. is $122.87
    C. is $147.45
    D. cannot be calculated from the facts given

22. The charge for 69,340 cubic feet of water at present   22._____

    A. is $69.34
    B. is $86.67
    C. is $104.01
    D. cannot be calculated from the facts given

23. The charge in 1981 for 87,420 cubic feet of water   23._____

    A. was $87.42
    B. was $133.13
    C. was $110.27
    D. cannot be calculated from the facts given

24. The charge in 1950 for 51,220 cubic feet of water   24._____

    A. was $51.22
    B. was $64.02
    C. was $76.83
    D. cannot be calculated from the facts given

25. A meter reads 81,400 cubic feet on January 1, 2007 and 21,800 cubic feet on January 1,   25._____
    2008.
    The charge for water consumed between the two readings

    A. is $60.60
    B. is $8940
    C. is $75.00
    D. cannot be calculated from the facts given

Questions 26-30.

DIRECTIONS: Answer questions 26 to 30 *only* on the basis of the information contained in
               the following paragraph.

The daily aggregate consumption of water within greater city averages 1117.1 million gallons daily, including the 70.8 million gallons daily furnished by the private water companies of County A and County This corresponds to a per capita consumption of 143.1 gallons per day. In addition to the foregoing, greater city-owned-and-operated public sources supply 24.1 millions gallons daily to communities outside greater city.

26. According to the above, the daily aggregate consumption of water within greater city from its public sources *only* is

   A. 70.8 million gallons daily
   B. 1046.3 million gallons daily
   C. 1117.1 million gallons daily
   D. not determinable from the information given

27. According to the above, the daily aggregate consumption of water both inside and outside greater city from its public sources *only* is:

   A. 24.1 million gallons daily
   B. 1070.4 million gallons daily
   C. 1117.1 million gallons daily
   D. not determinable from the information given

28. According to the above, the daily aggregate consumption of water both inside and outside greater city from its public sources and the private water companies of County A and B is

   A. 1046.3 million gallons daily
   B. 1070.4 million gallons daily
   C. 1141.2 million gallons daily
   D. not determinable from the information given

29. According to the above paragraph, the per capita consumption of water both inside and outside greater city from its public sources and the private water companies of County A and B is

   A. 24.1 gallons per day
   B. 143.1 gallons per day
   C. 167.2 gallons per day
   D. not determinable from the information given

30. According to the above paragraph, multiplying 143.1 by the population of greater city will give you

   A. the daily aggregate consumption of water within greater city
   B. the per capita consumption of water within greater city
   C. the daily aggregate consumption of water within greater city from its public sources only
   D. the daily aggregate consumption of water within greater city and from the private water companies of County A and B

Questions 31-35

DIRECTIONS: Answer questions 31 to 35 *only* on the basis of the information contained in the following paragraph.

No street shower shall be operated when the temperature is less than 80F, Street shower shall be operated between the hours of 10 M. and 8 P.M. only. Size of pipe connection to the shower head shall not exceed 1" in diameter. Not more than one street shower shall be operated within one block.

31. According to the above paragraph, the temperature at which a street shower may be operated is

    A. 40° F.   B. 60° F.   C. 70° F.   D. 90° F.

32. According to the above paragraph, the *one* of the following times at which a street shower may be operated is:

    A. 7:30 M.   B. 9:30 M.   C. 7:30 P.M.   D. 9:30 P.M.

33. According to the above paragraph, the *one* of the following sizes of pipe connections to the shower head which is permissible is:

    A. 1/2"   B. 1 1/4"   C. 1/4'   D. 3/4'

34. According to the above paragraph, the *maximum* number of street showers which can be operated within 3 blocks is:

    A. 1   B. 2   C. 3   D. 4

35. According to the above paragraph, the *one* of the following times and temperatures at which a street shower may be operated is:

    A. 9 A.M. and 79° F.
    B. 11 A.M. and 75° F.
    C. 12 noon and 85° F.
    D. 9 P.M. and 90° F.

Questions 36-40.

DIRECTIONS: Answer questions 36 to 40 *only* on the basis of the information contained in the following paragraph.

Meters shall be set or reset so that they may be easily examined and read. In all premises where the supply of water is to be fully metered, the meter shall be set within three feet of the building or vault wall at point of entry of service pipe. The service pipe between meter control valve and meter shall be kept exposed. When a building is situated back of the building line or conditions exist in a building that prevent the setting of the meter at a point of entry, meter may be set outside of the building in a proper watertight and frost-proof pit or meter box, or at other location approved by the Deputy Commissioner, Assistant to Commissioner, or Chief Inspector.

36. According to the above paragraph, meters shall be set

    A. in a location approved by Deputy Chief Inspector
    B. where they are protected from view
    C. where they can be easily examined and read
    D. within three feet of building or vault wall in premises where water charges are made on frontage basis only

37. According to the above paragraph, the part of service pipe that shall be kept exposed is that between the

    A. building line *and* point of entry
    B. meter box *and* frost-proof pit
    C. meter control valve *and* water
    D. vault wall *and* location approved by Commissioner

38. According to the above paragraph, in premises where the supply of water is to be fully metered, the one of the following distances from the building wall at point of entry of service pipe where meter can be set is

   A. 34"   B. 40"   C. 3 1/2 ft.   D. 2 yds.

39. According to the above paragraph, where a building is situated back of the building line, the one of the following locations where a meter may be set is

   A. in a location approved by Chief Inspector
   B. in a location approved by Deputy Chief Inspector
   C. inside of a building even if more than three feet from the building wall
   D. outside of the building in an open pit

40. From the above paragraph, it may be *inferred* that, of the following conditions, the one that will most likely damage a meter is

   A. enclosed control valve
   B. dryness and heat
   C. moisture and frost
   D. nearness to vault wall

41. One man can *impair* the work of a whole bureau. *Impair*, as used in this sentence, means, MOST NEARLY,

   A. improve   B. repair   C. replace   D. spoil

42. The inspector gave a *vivid* description of the violation. *Vivid*, as used in this sentence, means, MOST NEARLY,

   A. clear   B. long   C. short   D. true

43. A wrench was *utilized* in the job.
   Utilized, as used in this sentence, means, MOST NEARLY,

   A. abandoned   B. used   C. useless   D. moved

44. The pipe line *veered* to a new direction.
   Veered, as used in this sentence, means, MOST NEARLY,

   A. climbed   B. drove   C. sunk   D. turned

45. The tap size *exceeded* 4 inch.
   Exceeded, as used in this sentence, means, MOST NEARLY,

   A. almost reached
   B. equalled
   C. was less than
   D. was more than

46. The meter was *accessible*.
   Accessible, as used in this sentence means, MOST NEARLY,

   A. approachable
   B. blocked off
   C. broken
   D. legible

47. There was a *manifest* error in the meter. 47.____
    Manifest, as used in this sentence, means, MOST NEARLY,

    A. evident   B. large   C. small   D. theoretical

48. The inspector received a *commendation* for his courtesy. *Commendation,* as used in this 48.____
    sentence, means, MOST NEARLY,

    A. compliment   B. promotion   C. punishment   D. reproof

49. The weight of the meter *restricts* its use. *Restricts,* as used in this sentence, means, 49.____
    MOST NEARLY,

    A. allows   B. eliminates   C. insures   D. limits

50. The inspector's reputation was *vindicated. Vindicated,* as used in this sentence, means, 50.____
    MOST NEARLY,

    A. cleared   B. doubted   C. known   D. lost

KEY (CORRECT ANSWERS)

1. C	11. B	21. C	31. D	41. D
2. D	12. B	22. C	32. C	42. A
3. A	13. A	23. A	33. A	43. B
4. B	14. D	24. A	34. C	44. D
5. C	15. B	25. A	35. C	45. D
6. C	16. B	26. B	36. C	46. A
7. D	17. B	27. B	37. C	47. A
8. D	18. B	28. C	38. A	48. A
9. A	19. C	29. D	39. A	49. D
10. B	20. D	30. A	40. C	50. A

TEST 2

DIRECTIONS: Each question or incomplete statement is followed by several suggested answers or completions. Select the one that BEST answers the question or completes the statement. PRINT THE LETTER OF THE CORRECT ANSWER IN THE SPACE AT THE RIGHT.

1. A dripping faucet causes a water loss of 12 cubic feet out of every 320 cubic feet passed through the meter.
   The number of cubic feet wasted out of 3,680 cubic feet passed through the meter is

   A. 120   B. 132   C. 138   D. 144   1.____

2. If water flows through a 2" pipe at the rate of 1000 gallons per hour and through a 1" pipe exactly one quarter as fast, the number of hours it will take to fill a tank holding 10,000 gallons, with water flowing in both pipes, is

   A. 2   B. 4   C. 6   D. 8   2.____

3. Pipe A can fill a tank in 30 minutes, Pipe B in 45 minutes, and Pipe C in 90 minutes.
   The number of]minutes it will take *all* three pipes, running together, to fill the tank is

   A. 4   B. 6   C. 15   D. 30   3.____

4. A meter is tested by allowing water to flow through it into a rectangular tank. The tank is 6' long, 4' wide, and 5' high. The meter registeres 4734.7 cubic feet before the start of the test.
   If it is registering correctly, when the tank is full, it *will read*

   A. 4,764.7   B. N. 4,794.7   C. 4,854.7   D. 4,974.7   4.____

5. If water flows through a pipe at the rate of 24 gallons per minute, the number of gallons that will flow through in 1 hour and 15 minutes is

   A. 30   B. 1440   C. 1446   D. 1800   5.____

6. The units in which water meters usually record flow of water is

   A. cubic feet   B. cubic inches   C. gallons   D. liters   6.____

7. The number of cubic inches in a cubic foot is

   A. 12   B. 231   C. 746   D. 1728   7.____

8. The number of gallons of water in a cubic foot is, MOST NEARLY,

   A. 2   B. 4   C. 6 1/4   D. 7 1/2   8.____

9. The *minimum* dial capacity of an approved water meter in the city is, in cubic feet,

   A. 10,000   B. 1,000   C. 100,000   D. 500,000   9.____

10. On test, a meter registers one cubic foot for each 85/100th of a cubic foot of water that passes through it. The meter is   10.____

    A. over-registering
    B. under-registering
    C. registering within the allowable error
    D. registering correctly for water at 68F.

11. A meter is tested for registration accuracy by discharging water through the meter into a weighing tank.
    If the weight of 10 registered cubic feet is 674 lbs., the meter is

    A. over-registering
    B. under-registering
    C. registering correctly
    D. registering at one of the rates listed above but not determinable from the facts given

12. The type of meter which measures water by actual displacement is

    A. piston   B. rotometer   C. venturi   D. U-tube

13. The type of water meter which requires approval of certain officials of the department prior to installation, is the

    A. current
    B. disc
    C. piston
    D. oscillating piston

14. A compound water meter is BEST suited for service where the water flow

    A. is invariably small
    B. is invariably large
    C. varies, being sometimes small and sometimes large
    D. is either invariably small or invariably large

15. A meter is required where the minimum rate of water needed for the operation of air conditioning equipment exceeds, in gallon(s) per minute,

    A. 1/2   B. 6   C. 10   D. 15

16. The *maximum* size of current meters is *ordinarily*

    A. 12"   B. 24"   C. 36"   D. 48"

17. It is required that water can be metered which is used in the construction of buildings having a height of *at least* _____ story (stories).

    A. 1   B. 4   C. 7   D. 10

18. The type of meter which recores the flow of water by measuring velocity is the

    A. piston   B. simplex   C. U-tube   D. venturi

19. Water charges are collected by the

    A. board of water supply
    B. bureau of city collections
    C. bureau of water register
    D. comptroller's office

20. If a consumer fails to have a meter repaired within time, specified by a department order, the

    A. consumer will be guilty of a felony
    B. water charges will be made on fronta'ge basis
    C. water will be shut off
    D. work will be done by city plumbers at consumer's expense

21. Addition of chlorine to the drinking water supply of an office building

    A. is illegal under all conditions
    B. may be done with permit from the board of health
    C. may be done with permission of the commissioner of water supppy, gas and electricity
    D. may be done with permit from the bureau of water register

22. In water supply piping, a connection between the piping of one service with the piping of another is called a

    A. cross connection
    B. tap
    C. tee
    D. 3-way

23. A check valve is required in all services where

    A. a building is supplied by services connected to the same main
    B. offset swing joint is found to be insufficient
    C. repairs involve uncovering of tap
    D. there is possibility of backflow from tanks

24. Where water hammer conditions exist in any installation, it is necessary to install a(n)

    A. approved air chamber
    B. vacuum breaker
    C. tap in excess of that allowed on floor area basis
    D. suction tank

25. To prevent back siphonage, fixtures requiring submerged inlets should be equipped with

    A. cross connections   B. supply pipes
    C. tee connections   D. vacuum breakers

26. The one of the following which is approved is a(n)

    A. direct connection between water supply piping and drainage system
    B. flush tank operated by a ball cock with no vacuum breaker
    C. outside hose coupling for garden use
    D. approved vacuum breaker set at the flood level rim of a fixture

27. The pipe fitting used to connect a 1" pipe directly to a 1 1/4" pipe in the main line is called a

    A. 1 1/4" elbow   B. 1 1/4" x 1" reducer
    C. 1" sleeve   D. 1 1/4" union

28. A fitting used to make a right angle turn in a pipe line is called a(n)

    A. elbow   B. reducer   C. sleeve   D. union

29. The pipe fitting which is used to join two pieces of galvanized water pipe so as to permit opening them at the point of joining without cutting the pipe is called a(n)

    A. elbow   B. reducer   C. sleeve   D. union

30. A water connection on a pier used as a ship supply must be equipped with an approved

    A. ball valve
    B. cub stop
    C. horizontal swing check valve
    D. wet connection sleeve

31. It is *contrary* to regulations to install a curb valve

    A. in the service pipe   B. in a driveway
    C. on a fire service pipe   D. within 2 feet of the curb

32. Curb valves must be installed on all service pipes having a minimum diameter of *more* than

    A. 1"   B. 2"   C. 3"   D. 4"

33. That portion of the water pipe extending from the public main to the main house control valve inside building is called the

    A. plug
    B. service pipe
    C. tap
    D. wet connection

34. A service pipe shall be laid

    A. at least 4 ft. below street grade
    B. at 45 angle to street main
    C. by driving through the ground
    D. within 6 inches of another conduit

35. *Maximum* diameter of service pipe allowed for a 10" wet connection is

    A. 6"   B. 8"   C. 10"   D. 12"

36. The *one* of the following which may be used for service pipe larger than 2" in diameter is

    A. cast iron   B. copper   C. lead   D. lead alloy

37. *Minimum* size of service for a 4-family domestic building is

    A. 5/8"   B. 1"   C. 2 1/2"   D. 4"

38. Service pipes connected to taps 2" in diameter or larger must be at least

   A. 1" less than diameter of tap
   B. same size as tap
   C. 1" more than diameter of tap
   D. 1 1/2" in diameter

39. Where service pipe is 3" and tap diameter is 2", *minimum* size of gooseneck between service and tap is

   A. 3 3/4"   B. 1 1/2"   C. 2 1/2"   D. 2"

40. A connection to the city main may be made direct, without offset swing joint, when service pipe is made of

   A. brass   B. cast iron
   C. copper tubing   D. lead

41. A connection the same size as the main may be made to the city main by a

   A. Siamese   B. tap
   C. 3-way   D. wet connection

42. For factories or other large buildings, the type of connection to main that should be used is a

   A. Siamese   B. tap   C. 3-way   D. U-tube

43. A 2" or 3" connection may be made on a 4" main by a

   A. Siamese   B. tap
   C. 3-way   D. wet connection

44. The water meter that is approved for use in a 1-family residence in the city is:

   A. Eureka-Model B   B. American disc
   C. Hersey Torrent   D. Badger Turbine

45. The type of meter BEST adapted to measure accurately water for domestic consumption is the

   A. current   B. positive displacement
   C. U-tube   D. velocity

46. The type of meter BEST adapted to measure a large volume of water at a steady flow is the

   A. current   B. positive displacement
   C. mutating disc   D. rotary piston

47. The meter and connections from all supply tanks are shut off. The water from one open fixture, however, runs continuously.
   The *most logical* assumption is:

   A. The meter is defective
   B. There is another supply feeding the premises
   C. The running fixture needs a washer
   D. The supply tank is over-full

48. Taps are *generally* made of

   A. brass B. copper C. iron D. lead

49. Where the wall thickness of a pipe to be tapped is not sufficient to securely hold the tap, the plumber *must* provide a

   A. Siamese
   B. tapping saddle
   C. 3-way
   D. wet connection

50. If a meter is used on a cold water feed to a boiler, the *one* of the following that *should* be placed between the meter and the boiler is a

   A. check valve B. goose neck C. Siamese D. tap

KEY (CORRECT ANSWERS)

1. C	11. B	21. A	31. B	41. C
2. D	12. A	22. A	32. B	42. C
3. C	13. A	23. D	33. B	43. D
4. C	14. C	24. A	34. A	44. B
5. D	15. A	25. D	35. C	45. B
6. A	16. A	26. C	36. A	46. A
7. D	17. C	27. B	37. B	47. B
8. D	18. D	28. A	38. B	48. A
9. C	19. B	29. D	39. D	49. B
10. A	20. D	30. C	40. B	50. A

EXAMINATION SECTION
TEST 1

DIRECTIONS: Each question or incomplete statement is followed by several suggested answers or completions. Select the one that BEST answers the question or completes the statement. *PRINT THE LETTER OF THE CORRECT ANSWER IN THE SPACE AT THE RIGHT.*

1. The diameter of the tap *usually* determines the

    A. pressure in the main
    B. diameter of the service pipe
    C. size of the main
    D. size of the water meter

    1._____

2. Generally, the use of water is LEAST between the hours of

    A. 9 a.m. and 12 noon
    B. 1 a.m. to 4 a.m.
    C. 4 p.m. to 7 p.m.
    D. 6 a.m. to 9 a.m.

    2._____

3. The disease that is *most likely* to be spread by means of a polluted water supply is

    A. malaria
    B. cancer
    C. typhoid fever
    D. common cold

    3._____

4. Water demand load for commercial and industrial use is *usually* determined on the basis of the

    A. size of the water service pipe
    B. water pressure
    C. building floor area
    D. number of floors in the building

    4._____

5. Water consumption is measured by a water

    A. service pipe
    B. meter
    C. conduit
    D. tank

    5._____

6. The one of the following chemicals which is used to soften water is

    A. calcium sulphate
    B. magnesium carbonate
    C. sodium chloride
    D. slaked lime

    6._____

7. Unless there is an emergency or the department of water supply, gas and electricity gives permission, no hydrant shall be used when the temperature is less than 32 degrees Fahrenheit.
   The basis for this ruling is:

    A. This temperature is below the freezing point of water, resulting in freezing of hose connections
    B. Water freezes at this temperature

    7._____

C. The valve steam may crack at this temperature
D. The drip valve of the hydrant will not operate at this temperature, resulting in flooding of the hydrant

8. Using a hpse to water a lawn is usually forbidden from November 1 to March 31. The *most important* reason for this prohibition is to   8._____

    A. reduce unnecessary use of water
    B. avoid hazards due to ice formation on the lawn
    C. avoid freezing of the water in the hose
    D. avoid dangerous reduction in water main pressure

9. A building is equipped with a one-inch water meter. The size refers to the   9._____

    A. inside diameter of the meter inlet pipe
    B. diameter of the meter disc
    C. loss of head in inches
    D. maximum flow in cubic inches per second

10. A bibb seat reamer is *most probably* required when   10._____

    A. a faucet is leaking
    B. a hose cannot be screwed tightly to a hose bib
    C. there is a burr on the inside of the cur pipe
    D. a tap has become plugged

11. If there is a constant leak from a flush tank into the bowl of a water closet, it is *probably* due to   11._____

    A. the ball cock jammed shut
    B. lift wire disconnected from the handle lever
    C. a hole in the copper float
    D. a defective shut-off valve

12. When a building is to be altered or erected, the water used in construction is   12._____

    A. metered if the building is more than six stories high
    B. metered if the building is less than six stories high
    C. not metered unless the building is eight or more stories high
    D. not metered if the building is to be used for dwelling purposes

13. With reference to water supply, the term "peak load" *usually* refers to: 13._____

    A. Height of structures to be supplied with water
    B. Elevation of water supply
    C. Rate of maximum demand
    D. Capacity of pressure regulating valves

14. A cubic foot of water is equal to about _____ gallons.   14._____

    A. 5 1/4   B. 7 1/2   C. 6   D. 8 1/2

15. One pound per square inch pressure of water will raise water to a height of 15.____

    A. 2.3 feet B. 18 inches
    C. 14.7 feet D. 4.5 feet

16. When the hub end of a soil pipe is to be sealed off, the *proper* fitting to use is a 16.____

    A. lug B. saddle
    C. cap D. plug

17. In water piping work, the term "riser" refers to 17.____

    A. a horizontal supply line
    B. hot water lines only
    C. cold water lines only
    D. a vertical supply line

18. The purpose of a check valve is to 18.____

    A. check excessive pressure of water
    B. allow water to flow one way only
    C. prevent sediment from backing into service pipe
    D. check trapped air in water pipe

19. The thread of a pipe with a male thread is 19.____

    A. on the inside of the pipe
    B. on the outside of the pipe
    C. inside and outside the pipe
    D. less likely to be damaged than the thread of a pipe with a female thread

20. Resistance to flow of water is *least* in a(n) 20.____

    A. angle valve B. pressure reducing valve
    C. globe valve D. gate valve

Questions 21 - 22.

Questions 21 and 22 are based on the following diagram.

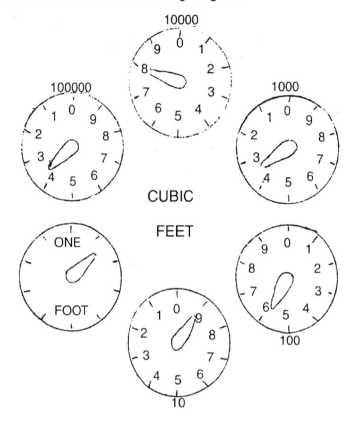

21. The water meter reading shown in the sketch, in cubic feet, is

   A. 373,591   B. 68,449   C. 37,359   D. 173,359

21.____

22. The pointer which does not appear in a correct position is on the dial labeled

   A. 1,000   B. 10,000   C. 10   D. 100

22.____

23. Assume that the current meter reading on the meter used in Question 21 is 8,947 cubic feet. The last reading was 81,732 cubic feet.
    It is obvious that

   A. consumption amounted to 72,785 feet
   B. the meter has been tampered with
   C. the meter is not recording properly
   D. consumption amounted to 27,215 cubic feet

23.____

24. Hot water meters should *not* be used on cold water lines because they

   A. will not measure cold water flows accurately
   B. will be injured by cold water flow
   C. cost far more than cold water meters
   D. are designed for intermittent water flows and not for a continuous supply

24.____

25. In an inspection of a water meter, it is found that the meter seals have been tampered with. The inspector should

   A. take the meter reading and then report the matter to his superior
   B. discuss the matter with the user and then warn him that the water supply may be shut off
   C. determine probable usage during the current period and then reset the meter to give an appropriate reading
   D. shut the inlet valve, place a seal upon it, and report the matter to his superior

26. An inspector finds that a water supply connection has been made to a house service pipe at a point between the basement wall and the water meter. This will result in

   A. contamination of the water supply
   B. excessive meter readings
   C. meter readings less than actual consumption
   D. waste of water

Questions 27 - 31.

Questions 27 to 31 refer to the diagram below.

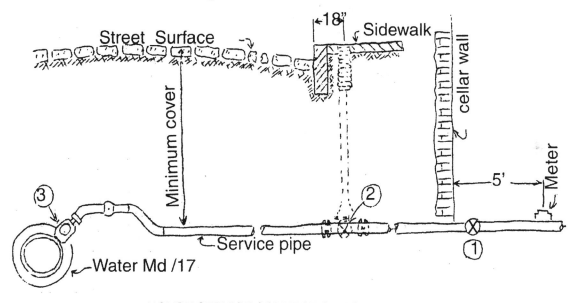

HOUSE SERVICE CONNECTION TO WATER MAIN

27. The device numbered (1) in the diagram is *probably* a _____ valve.

   A. check   B. foot
   C. gate   D. angle

28. The minimum cover for service pipe is specified as 4 feet. The *most important* reason for this requirement is to

   A. prevent freezing of water in service pipe
   B. avoid tampering with water supply or possible pollution of service line
   C. provide proper drainage in case of a leak
   D. provide a firm backfill to avoid breaking of connection between the water main and service pipe

29. Item numbered (2) in the diagram is a(n) 29.____

   A. corporation cock
   B. curb cock
   C. angle valve
   D. pressure reducing valve

30. Item numbered (3) in the diagram is a 30.____

   A. reducer   B. reducing flange
   C. corporation cock   D. service tee

31. Assume that a leak in the house service has been located in the pipe line beneath the sidewalk near the building line. To stop any further water loss until repairs are made, the *proper* procedure to follow is to close 31.____

   A. the valve at (1)
   B. the valve at (2)
   C. valves on the water main from which the service pipe leads
   D. all water outlets in the building

32. Each new service pipe shall be laid in a straight line at right angles to the street main. The BEST reason for this requirement is that it 32.____

   A. minimizes leakage at joints
   B. simplifies location of the service pipe under the sidewalk
   C. requires the shortest length of pipe
   D. permits the greatest flow of water

33. Water is flowing into a cylindrical tank at the rate of four cubic feet per minute. The time it will take to fill the tank whose dimensions are seven feet in height and four feet in diameter is *about* 33.____

   A. 22 minutes   B. one-half hour
   C. 15 minutes   D. one hour

34. The term "head" as used in relation to the flow of water can also be expressed as 34.____

   A. rate of flow
   B. resistance of pipe to water flow
   C. gallons per second
   D. water pressure

35. The flow of water in a pipe in cubic feet per second is equal to the 35.____

   A. diameter of the pipe in feet multiplied by the velocity in feet per second
   B. area of the pipe in square feet divided by the rate of flow in feet per second
   C. diameter of the pipe in feet divided by rate of flow in feet per second
   D. area of the pipe in square feet multiplied by the velocity in feet per second

36. To check a water meter to see whether it is registering, the procedure to follow is to 36.____

   A. turn the water off
   B. check the movement of the pointer of the dial of highest capacity
   C. check the movement of the pointer of the dial of lowest capacity
   D. remove the face of the meter to see if the gears are in motion

Questions 37 - 38.

Questions 37 and 38 are based upon the diagram below.

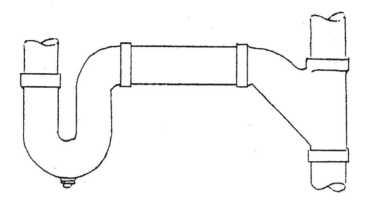

37. The trap shown in the diagram is *commonly* called a

    A. P-trap
    B. s-trap
    C. mechanical trap
    D. Y-trap

37._____

38. The function of this trap is to

    A. prevent inflow of air into soil pipe
    B. prevent backflow of sewer gas
    C. collect all wastes in the bottom of the trap
    D. prevent water from backing up into the water fixture

38._____

39. The purpose of a float and float switch in a roof tank is to

    A. keep the tank full
    B. close off the roof supply when water pressure is low
    C. vary pressure with the demand of the lower floors
    D. provide water for fire protection

39._____

40. The average pressure of water in the water mains in the city is *about* _____ lbs. per square inch.

    A. 50   B. 25   C. 95   D. 18

40._____

Questions 41 - 45.

The fittings represented in Column I on the following page are commonly found in water supply lines in a building. Select the correct name from Column II for the fitting in Column I and place the letter representing your choice next to the number of the fitting on your answer sheet.

8 (#1)

Column I	Column II
41.	A. bushing
	B. union
	C. coupling
42.	D. cap
	E. plug
	F. nipple
43.	G. reducer
44.	
45.	

41.____

42.____

43.____

44.____

45.____

46. Where a meter is used to measure water consumption, the charge for water is   46.____

    A. fifteen cents per hundred cubic feet
    B. fifteen cents per thousand cubic feel
    C. $1.50 per hundred cubic feet
    D. seventy-five cents per hundred cubic feet

47. The discs of positive displacement-type water meters are *usually* made of   47.____

    A. hardwood   B. metal alloys
    C. hard rubber   D. bronze

48. After you have read a meter, the owner tells you that he will be unable to pay the bill on time and asks you what will happen.   48.____
You *should* tell him that

    A. you just read the meter; after that, it is up to the office
    B. you will report the matter to your superior
    C. if he fails to pay before the end of next month he will be charged interest on the bill
    D. the city's financial position is not good and he should make every effort to pay the bill

49. You find that the meter glass is so dirty that the meter cannot be read. Department regulations provide that

    A. the supply shall be shut off until the meter is placed in good order
    B. the glass will be cleaned and leaky spindles packed without charge
    C. the meter be removed and replaced temporarily by a straight piece of pipe
    D. the owner be fined because the meter was allowed to become unsuitable

Questions 50 - 51.

Questions 50 and 51 are based on the table of frontage rates listed below.
The annual frontage rents on premises wholly or partly unmetered shall be as follows:

Front Width of Building:	One-Story
16 feet and under	$ 6.00
Over 16 feet, up to and including 18 feet	7.50
Over 18 feet, up to and including 20	9.00
Over 20 feet, up to and including 22 1/2 feet	10.50
Over 22 1/2 feet, up to and including 25 feet	12.00
Over 25 feet, up to and including 30 feet	15.00
Over 30 feet, up to and including 37 1/2 feet	18.00
Over 37 1/2 feet, up to and including 50 feet	21.00

For each additional story $1.50 per annum shall be added; and for each additional ten (10) feet or part thereof above fifty (50) feet in front width of building, #3 shall be added.

The apportionment of the regular frontage rates upon buildings shall be on the basis that but one family is to occupy same, and for each additional family or apartment, $1.50 per year shall be charged.

Baths in excess of one (1) to each house, $4.50 per annum.

Shower bath, not installed over bath tubs, and "sitz" baths shall be charged same as baths.

50. Based on the above data, the annual water charge for a 2-story, 1-family dwelling, 20 feet wide, is

    A. $9.00   B. $10.50   C. $13.50   D. $15.00

51. Based on the above data, the annual water charge for a 2-story, 1-family dwelling, 24 feet wide, is

    A. $12.00   B. $13.50   C. $16.30   D. $18.00

52. Gaskets are *usually* used to

    A. make caulked joints leak-proof
    B. seal threaded joints
    C. make flanged joints pressure tight
    D. reduce possible breaking of joints due to water hammer pressure

53. The fitting used to close off the threaded male end of a line is a

    A. bushing
    B. union
    C. plug
    D. cap

54. To take a right-angle line from a horizontal or vertical run of pipe, the fitting to use is a

    A. tee
    B. 90° elbow
    C. 60 Y-bend
    D. cross

55. An inspector is told by the owner of a factory that his water bill is excessive and that his use of water was about the same as the previous year when the bill was lower. The inspector *should*

    A. make an immediate floor-to-floor survey to detect sources of water waste
    B. suggest a waste survey by the owner or his plumber
    C. suggest that the owner's statement is probably not correct, as evidenced by the meter reading
    D. suggest that a new meter by installed

56. An additional toilet has been installed in the basement of a small private residence. It is *correct* to say that water charges will

    A. *not* be changed unless there is an increased use of water
    B. be increased because an additional fixture has been installed
    C. be changed only if such installation is the result of an increase in the number of inhabitants of the dwelling
    D. *not* be changed because such buildings usually have a metered supply

Questions 57 - 59.

Questions 57 to 59 inclusive refer to the paragraph below.

Part of a section of the Administrative Code relating to the placing of water meters ptates:

"This section shall not be CONSTRUED so as to REMIT or prevent the due collection of arrearages or charges for water consumption heretofore INCURRED, nor interfere with the proper liens therefor, nor of charges, or rates, or liens hereafter incurred for water consumption in any building or place which may not contain one of the meters aforesaid."

57. The word "construed" underlined in this paragraph means, *most nearly*,

    A. delayed
    B. mistaken
    C. enacted
    D. interpreted

58. The word "remit" as used in this paragraph means, *most nearly*,

    A. send out
    B. dispense with
    C. settle
    D. justify

59. The word "incurred" underlined in this paragraph means, *most nearly*,

    A. credited with
    B. discharged
    C. accounted for
    D. liable for

60. While making a meter reading, an inspector notices some defects in the water supply line. He suggests corrections to the property owner. The grateful owner insists that the inspector accept a gratuity.
The inspector *should*

    A. accept the gratuity with the understanding that the money will be forwarded to the city treasurer
    B. accept the gratuity since he has assisted the owner beyond his regular duty
    C. refuse the gratuity because acceptance is a violation of department regulations
    D. refuse the gratuity because acceptance would mean that he has not taken a proper reading

60.____

61. An inspector, sent to obtain meter readings, is refused admission to the premises.
His *next* step should be to

    A. recommend that the water supply to the premises be shut off
    B. report the refusal to his superior for further action
    C. obtain the assistance of the police to force access to the meter
    D. recommend using the average consumption for the last three periods to determine the current charge

61.____

62. A tenant informs an inspector of water consumption that there is a definite hazard due to leakage of illuminating gas in the hallway and cellar of the building. The *most appropriate* procedure to follow is to

    A. advise the tenant that the owner will be informed of the possible hazard
    B. tell the tenant that he has no jurisdiction
    C. make a soap test to locate the gas leak
    D. notify the Police Department, advising them of the situation

62.____

63. An inspection of a tenant's complaint reveals several neglected leaks in water supply fixtures and lines. The, owner of the small tenement building tells you that he'll take care of the matter in due time and that, since he is paying for the water used in the form of water taxes, it is not really your concern. Your answer *should be* that

    A. the water tax will be increased if the waste caused by the leaks is not corrected
    B. the water supply may be contaminated through leakage
    C. his statement is correct, but that the water is being wasted nevertheless
    D. his statement is not correct, since his water supply is not metered

63.____

64. An inspector notices a sawed-off shotgun in the basement of an office building. This is an illegal weapon and no permits are issued by the Police Department for its use.
The inspector *should*

    A. notify the building superintendent of his discovery
    B. ignore the gun, since he has no jurisdiction at all
    C. notify the local precinct station of the Police Department
    D. send a report about the gun to the main office of the department of water supply, gas and electricity

64.____

65. An inspector, who has just completed an inspection, is stopped on the street by a man who asks him for information about the economic status of the owner and the condition of the property.
The inspector's action *should be* to

    A. cooperate with this man and give him the desired information to the best of his knowledge
    B. refer the man to the main office for the desired information
    C. suggest that the man discuss the matter with the owner himself
    D. tell him about the condition of the property and refer him to the nearest commercial bank for information as to the owner's economic status

66. The *most important* reason for avoiding the use of lead pipe for water supply lines in a building is that it

    A. tends to sag and become deformed
    B. cracks easily in cold weather
    C. interferes with flow due to formation of lead compounds
    D. is corroded readily by electrolysis

67. The new owner of a small residence writes to the department of water supply, gas and electricity asking for a refund since he was away from home during the summer months. His request was denied.
The *basis* for the denial of refund is:

    A. The water charge is fixed as of conditions on January 1, and is valid for the entire year whether the water is used or not
    B. The water charge may not be refunded in part unless the owner filed a formal notice and had the service connection sealed off
    C. There is no way of determining how much water was actually used during the year
    D. Water waste might have occurred during the period the dwelling was closed

68. A person who intends to close his house for three months during the summer should

    A. notify the department
    B. make a waste survey before so doing
    C. shut off the main house control valve
    D. do nothing if all fixtures are in good repair

69. In your inspection of a house you notice that a faucet is leaking.
Of the following, the *most probable* cause for the leak is:

    A. uneven seat
    B. corrosion of the supply pipe
    C. excessive water pressure
    D. too little water pressure

70. The opening of a faucet extends below the overflow of a wash basin. The *principal* objection to this type of fixture is that

    A. the faucet end may become polluted
    B. water hammer is possible if the faucet is open when the basin is full
    C. back-siphonage is possible when the faucet is open and the basin is full
    D. a careless user is more likely to waste water

71. A meter may not be installed if it is more than one standard size larger than the tap or connection to the water main.
   The *reason* for this requirement is that

   A. if the meter is more than one standard size larger than the connection, it may not register small flows accurately
   B. the connection of a larger meter will result in higher friction losses
   C. the flow of water in the service pipe will be greatly increased
   D. too great a difference between the size of the supply line and the meter inlet makes connection difficult

72. A faucet in the basement of a tenement is leaking. Before this faucet can be repaired, it is *necessary* to shut off

   A. the service line where it enters the building
   B. all valves between the street and the faucet
   C. valve on the riser above the faucet
   D. the valve below the faucet

73. While reading a meter in a factory you hear much banging in the supply line. The superintendent tells you that the banging has been going on ever since flushometers were installed in the rest rooms.
   Department regulations require that

   A. the piping layout be altered to eliminate the noise
   B. nothing need be done
   C. the flushometers be removed
   D. an air chamber be installed

74. On an inspection of a meter in a commercial building, you see a man in the basement working on an oil burner. You do not know his identity or whether he is authorized to work in the building.
   The *most reasonable* thing to do is to

   A. pay no attention to the man and take the meter reading
   B. ignore him, but include a brief statement about him in your report
   C. challenge the man and obtain his identity
   D. watch him carefully to determine if his behavior is proper

75. The department of water supply, gas and electricity operates a high pressure fire system in some locations so that

   A. water may be available for fire fighting in areas of low elevation
   B. the water used for fire fighting will not freeze under high pressure
   C. manufacturing, business and waterfront sections may have extra protection
   D. water may be available for fire fighting in sections of high elevation

KEY (CORRECT ANSWERS)

1. D	16. D	31. B	46. A	61. B
2. B	17. D	32. B	47. C	62. D
3. C	18. B	33. A	48. C	63. C
4. A	19. B	34. D	49. B	64. C
5. B	20. D	35. D	50. B	65. C
6. D	21. C	36. C	51. D	66. A
7. B	22. B	37. A	52. C	67. A
8. A	23. D	38. B	53. D	68. C
9. A	24. A	39. A	54. A	69. A
10. A	25. A	40. A	55. B	70. C
11. C	26. C	41. D	56. B	71. A
12. A	27. B	42. C	57. D	72. D
13. C	28. A	43. F	58. B	73. D
14. B	29. B	44. A	59. D	74. A
15. A	30. C	45. B	60. C	75. C

ARITHMETIC
EXAMINATION SECTION
TEST 1

DIRECTIONS: Each question or incomplete statement is followed by several suggested answers or completions. Select the one that *BEST* answers the question or completes the statement. *PRINT THE LETTER OF TEE CORRECT ANSWER IN THE SPACE AT THE RIGHT.*

1. Add $4.34, $34.50, $6.00, $101.76, $90.67. From the result, subtract $60.54 and $10,56. 1.____
   A. $76.17   B. $156.37   C. $166.17   D. $300.37

2. Add 2,200, 2,600, 252 and 47.96. From the result, subtract 202.70, 1,200, 2,150 and 434.43. 2.____
   A. 1,112.83   B. 1,213.46   C. 1,341.51   D. 1,348.91

3. Multiply 1850 by .05 and multiply 3300 by .08 and, then, add both results, 3.____
   A. 242.50   B. 264,00   C. 333.25   D. 356.50

4. Multiply 312.77 by .04. Round off the result to the nearest hundredth. 4.____
   A. 12.52   B. 12.511   C. 12.518   D. 12.51

5. Add 362.05, 91.13, 347.81 and 17.46 and then divide the result by 6. The answer, rounded off to the nearest hundredth, is: 5.____
   A. 138.409   B. 137.409   C. 136.41   D. 136.40

6. Add 66.25 and 15.06 and, then, multiply the result by 2 1/6. The answer is, most nearly, 6.____
   A. 176.18   B. 176.17   C. 162.66   D. 162.62

7. Each of the following items contains three decimals. In which case do *all* three decimals have the *SAME* value? 7.____
   A. .3; .30; .03
   B. .25; .250; .2500
   C. 1.9; 1.90;1.09
   D. .35; .350; .035

8. Add 1/2 the sum of (539.84 and 479.26) to 1/3 the sum of (1461.93 and 927.27). Round off the result to the nearest whole number. 8.____
   A. 3408   B. 2899   C. 1816   D. 1306

9. Multiply $5,906.09 by 15% and, then, divide the result by 3 and round off to the nearest cent. 9.____
   A. $295.30   B. $885.91   C. $2,657.74   D. $29,530.45

10. Multiply 630 by 517. 10.____
    A. 325,710   B. 345,720   C. 362,425   D. 385,660

11. Multiply 35 by 846.

    A. 4050   B. 9450   C. 18740   D. 29610

12. Multiply 823 by 0.05.

    A. 0.4115   B. 4.115   C. 41.15   D. 411.50

13. Multiply 1690 by 0.10.

    A. 0.169   B. .1.69   C. 16.90   D. 169.0

14. Divide 2765 by 35.

    A. 71   B. 79   C. 87   D. 93

15. From $18.55 subtract $6.80.

    A. $9.75   B. $10.95   C. $11.75   D. $25.35

16. The sum of 2.75 + 4.50 + 3.60 is:

    A. 9.75   B. 10.85   C. 11.15   D. 11.95

17. The sum of 9.63 + 11.21 + 17.25 is:

    A. 36.09   B. 38.09   C. 39.92   D. 41.22

18. The sum of 112.0 + 16.9 + 3.84 is:

    A. 129.3   B. 132.74   C. 136.48   D. 167.3

19. When 65 is added to the result of 14 multiplied by 13, the answer is:

    A. 92   B. 182   C. 247   D. 16055

20. From $391.55 subtract $273.45.

    A. $118.10   B. $128.20   C. $178.10   D. $218.20

KEY (CORRECT ANSWERS)

1.	C	11.	D
2.	A	12.	C
3.	D	13.	D
4.	D	14.	B
5.	C	15.	C
6.	B	16.	B
7.	B	17.	B
8.	D	18.	B
9.	C	19.	C
10.	A	20.	A

SOLUTIONS TO PROBLEMS

1. ($4.34 + $34.50 + $6.00 + $101.76 + $90.67) - ($60.54 + $10.56) = $237.27 - $71.10 = $166.17.

2. (2200 + 2600 + 252 + 47.96) - (202.70 + 1200 + 2150 + 434.43) = 5099.96 - 3987.13 = 1112.83

3. (1850)(.05) + (3300)(.08) = 92.5 + 264 = 356.50

4. (312.77)(.04) = 12.5108 = 12.51 to nearest hundredth

5. $(362.05+91.13+347.81+17.46) \div 6 = 136.408\overline{3} = 136.41$ to nearest hundredth

6. $(66.25+15.06)(2\frac{1}{6}) = 176.171\overline{6} \approx 176.17$

7. .25 = .250 = .2500

8. $(\frac{1}{2})(539.84+479.26) + \frac{1}{3}(1461.93+927.27) = 509.55 + 796.4 = 1305.95 = 1306$ nearest whole number

9. ($5906.09)(.15) ÷ 3 = ($885.9135)/3 = 295.3045 = $295.30 to nearest cent

10. (630)(517) = 325,710

11. (35)(846) = 29,610

12. (823)(.05) = 41.15

13. (1690)(10) = 169.0

14. 2765 ÷ 3.5 = 79

15. $18.55 - $6.80 = $11.75

16. 2.75 + 4.50 + 3.60 = 10.85

17. 9.63 + 11.21 + 17.25 = 38.09

18. 112.0 + 16.9 + 3.84 = 132.74

19. 65 + (14)(13) = 65 + 182 = 247

20. $391.55 - $273.45 = $118.10

TEST 2

DIRECTIONS   Each question or incomplete statement is followed by several suggested answers or completions. Select the one that *BEST* answers the question or completes the statement. *PRINT THE LETTER OF TEE CORRECT ANSWER IN THE SPACE AT THE RIGHT.*

1. The sum of $29.61 + $101.53 + $943.64 is: 1.____
   A. $983.88   B. $1074.78   C. $1174.98   D. $1341.42

2. The sum of $132.25 + $85.63 + $7056,44 is: 2.____
   A. $1694.19   B. $7274.32   C. $8464.57   D. $9346.22

3. The sum of 4010 + 1271 + 838 + 23 is: 3.____
   A. 6142   B. 6162   C. 6242   D. 6362

4. The sum of 53632 + 27403 + 98765 + 75424 is: 4.____
   A. 19214   B. 215214   C. 235224   D. 255224

5. The sum of 76342 + 49050 + 21206 + 59989 is: 5.____
   A. 196586   B. 206087   C. 206587   D. 234487

6. The sum of $452.13 + $963.45 + $621.25 is: 6.____
   A. $1936.83   B. $2036.83   C. $2095.73   D. $2135.73

7. The sum of 36392 + 42156 + 98765 is: 7.____
   A. 167214   B. 177203   C. 177313   D. 178213

8. The sum of 40125 + 87123 + 24689 is: 8.____
   A. 141827   B. 151827   C. 151937   D. 161947

9. The sum of 2379 + 4015 + 6521 + 9986 is: 9.____
   A. 22901   B. 22819   C. 21801   D. 21791

10. From 50962 subtract 36197.   10.____
    A. 14675   B. 14765   C. 14865   D. 24765

11. From 90000 subtract 31928.   11.____
    A. 58072   B. 59062   C. 68172   D. 69182

12. From 63764 subtract 21548.   12.____
    A. 42216   B. 43122   C. 45126   D. 85312

13. From $9605.13 subtract $2715.96.   13.____
    A. $12,321.09   B. $8,690.16   C. $6,990.07   D. $6,889.17

14. From 76421 subtract 73101. 14.____
    A. 3642   B. 3540   C. 3320   D. 3242

15. From $8.25 subtract $6.50. 15.____
    A. $1.25   B. $1.50   C. $1.75   D. $2.25

16. Multiply 583 by 0.50. 16.____
    A. $291.50   B. 28.15   C. 2.815   D. 0.2815

17. Multiply 0.35 by 1045. 17.____
    A. 0.36575   B. 3.6575   C. 36.575   D. 365.75

18. Multiply 25 by 2513. 18.____
    A. 62825   B. 62725   C. 60825   D. 52825

19. Multiply 423 by 0.01. 19.____
    A. 0.0423   B. 0.423   C. 4.23   D. 42.3

20. Multiply 6.70 by 3.2. 20.____
    A. 2.1440   B. 21.440   C. 214.40   D. 2144.0

KEY (CORRECT ANSWERS)

1. B   11. A
2. B   12. A
3. A   13. D
4. D   14. C
5. C   15. C

6. B   16. A
7. C   17. D
8. C   18. A
9. A   19. C
10. B   20. B

SOLUTIONS TO PROBLEMS

1. $29.61 + $101.53 + $943.64 = $1074.78

2. $132.25 + $85.63 + $7056.44 = $7274.32

3. 4010 + 1271 + 838 + 23 = 6142

4. 53,632 + 27,403 + 98,765 + 75,424 = 255,224

5. 76,342 + 49,050 + 21,206 + 59,989 = 206,587

6. $452.13 + $963.45 + $621.25 = $2036.83

7. 36,392 + 42,156 + 98,765 = 177,313

8. 40,125 + 87,123 + 24,689 = 151,937

9. 2379 + 4015 + 6521 + 9986 = 22,901

10. 50962 - 36197 = 14,765

11. 90,000 - 31,928 = 58,072

12. 63,764 - 21,548 = 42,216

13. $9605.13 - $2715.96 = $6889.17

14. 76,421 - 73,101 = 3320

15. $8.25 - $6.50 = $1.75

16. (583)(.50) = 291.50

17. (.35)(1045) = 365.75

18. (25)(2513) = 62,825

19. (423)(.01) = 4.23

20. (6.70)(3.2) = 21.44

TEST 3

DIRECTIONS: Each question or incomplete statement is followed by several suggested answers or completions. Select the one that BEST answers the question or completes the statement. *PRINT THE LETTER OF TEE CORRECT ANSWER IN THE SPACE AT THE RIGHT.*

Questions 1-4.

DIRECTIONS: For each of Questions 1-4, perform the indicated arithmetic and choose the correct answer from among the four choices given.

1. 12.485
   + 347

   A. 12,038   B. 12,128   C. 12,782   D. 12,832

2. 74,137
   + 711

   A. 74,326   B. 74,848   C. 78,028   D. .D. 78,926

3. 3,749
   - 671

   A. 3,078   B. 3,168   C. 4,028   D. 4,420

4. 19,805
   -18904

   A. 109   B. 901   C. 1,109   D. 1,901

5. When 119 is subtracted from the sum of 2016 + 1634, the remainder is:
   A. 2460   B. 3531   C. 3650   D. 3769

6. Multiply 35 X 65 X 15.
   A. 2275   B. 24265   C. 31145   D. 34125

7. 90% expressed as a decimal is:
   A. .009   B. .09   C. .9   D. 9.0

8. Seven-tenths of a foot expressed in inches is:
   A. 5.5   B. 6.5   C. 7   D. 8.4

9. If 95 men were divided into crews of five men each, the *number* of crews that will be formed is:
   A. 16   B. 17   C. 18   D. 19

10. If a man earns $19.50 an hour, the *number* of working hours it will take him to earn $4,875 is, most nearly,

    A. 225　　　B. 250　　　C. 275　　　D. 300

11. If 5 1/2 loads of gravel cost $55.00, then 6 1/2 loads will cost:

    A. $60.　　　B. $62.50　　　C. $65.　　　D. $66.00

12. At $2.50 a yard, 27 yards of concrete will cost:

    A. $36.　　　B. $41.80　　　C. $54.　　　D. $67.50

13. A distance is measured and found to be 52.23 feet. In feet and inches, this distance is, most nearly, 52 feet *and*

    A. 2 3/4"　　　B. 3 1/4"　　　C. 3 3/4"　　　D. 4 1/4"

14. If a maintainer gets $5.20 per hour and time and one-half for working over 40 hours, his *gross* salary for a week in which he worked 43 hours would be

    A. $208.00　　　B. $223.60　　　C. $231.40　　　D. $335.40

15. The circumference of a circle is given by the formula C = ΠD, where C is the circumference, D is the diameter, and Π is about 3 1/7.
    If a coil is 15 turns of steel cable has an average diameter of 20 inches, the *total* length of cable on the coil is *nearest* to

    A. 5 feet　　　B. 78 feet　　　C. 550 feet　　　D. 943 feet

16. The measurements of a poured concrete foundation show that 54 cubic feet of concrete have been placed.
    If payment for this concrete is to be on the basis of cubic yards, the 54 cubic feet must be

    A. multiplied by 27　　　B. multiplied by 3
    C. divided by 27　　　D. divided by 3

17. If the cost of 4 1/2 tons of structural steel is $1,800, then the cost of 12 tons is, most nearly,

    A. $4,800　　　B. $5,400　　　C. $7,200　　　D. $216,000

18. An hourly-paid employee working 12:00 midnight to 8:00 a.m. is directed to report to the medical staff for a physical examination at 11:00 a.m. of the same day.
    The pay allowed him for reporting will be an extra

    A. 1 hour　　　B. 2 hours　　　C. 3 hours　　　D. 4 hours

19. The *total* length of four pieces of 2" pipe, whose lengths are 7' 3 1/2", 4' 2 3/16", 5' 7 5/16", and 8' 5 7/8", respectively, is:

    A. 24' 6 3/4"　　　B. 24' 7 15/16"
    C. 25' 5 13/16"　　　D. 25' 6 7/8"

20. As a senior mortuary caretaker, you are preparing a monthly report, using the following figures: 20.____

    No. of bodies received   983
    No. of bodies claimed   720
    No. of bodies sent to city cemetery   14
    No. of bodies sent to medical schools   9

How many bodies remained at the end of the monthly reporting period?

   A.   230   B.   240   C.   250   D.   260

KEY (CORRECT ANSWERS)

1.	D	11.	C
2.	B	12.	D
3.	A	13.	A
4.	B	14.	C
5.	B	15.	B
6.	D	16.	C
7.	C	17.	A
8.	D	18.	C
9.	D	19.	D
10.	B	20.	B

SOLUTIONS TO PROBLEMS

1. 12,485 + 347 = 12,832

2. 74,137 + 711 = 74,848

3. 3749 - 671 = 3078

4. 19,805 - 18,904 = 901

5. (2016 + 1634) - 119 = 3650 - 119 = 3531

6. (35)(65)(15) = 34,125

7. 90% = .90 or .9

8. $(\frac{7}{10})(12) = 8.4$ inches

9. 95 ÷ 5 = 19 crews

10. $4875 ÷ $19.50 = 250 days

11. Let x = cost. Then, $\frac{5\frac{1}{2}}{6\frac{1}{2}} = \frac{\$55.00}{x}$. $5\frac{1}{2} = 357.50$. Solving, x = $65

12. ($2.50)(27) = $67.50

13. .23-ft. = 2.76 in., so 52.23 ft ≈ 52 ft. $2\frac{3}{4}$ in. (.76 ≈ $\frac{3}{4}$)

14. Salary = ($5.20)(40) + ($7.80)(3) = $231.40

15. Length ≈ $(15)(3\frac{1}{7})(20)$ ≈ 943 in. ≈ 78 ft.

16. There are 27 cu.ft. in 1 cu.yd. To change from 54 cu.ft. to cu.yds., divide by 27.

17. $1800 ÷ $4\frac{1}{2}$ = = $400 per ton. Then, 12 tons cost ($400)(12) = $4800

18. Instead of working 12 to 8, he will be staying until 11 AM, an extra 3 hours.

19. $7'3\frac{1}{2}" + 4'2\frac{3}{16}" + 5'7\frac{5}{16}" + 8'5\frac{7}{8}" = 24'17\frac{30}{16}" = 24'18\frac{7}{8}"$

20. 983 - 720 - 14 - 9 = 240 bodies left.

ARITHMETICAL REASONING
EXAMINATION SECTION
TEST 1

DIRECTIONS: Each question or incomplete statement is followed by several suggested answers or completions. Select the one that BEST answers the question or completes the statement. *PRINT THE LETTER OF THE CORRECT ANSWER IN THE SPACE AT THE RIGHT.*

1.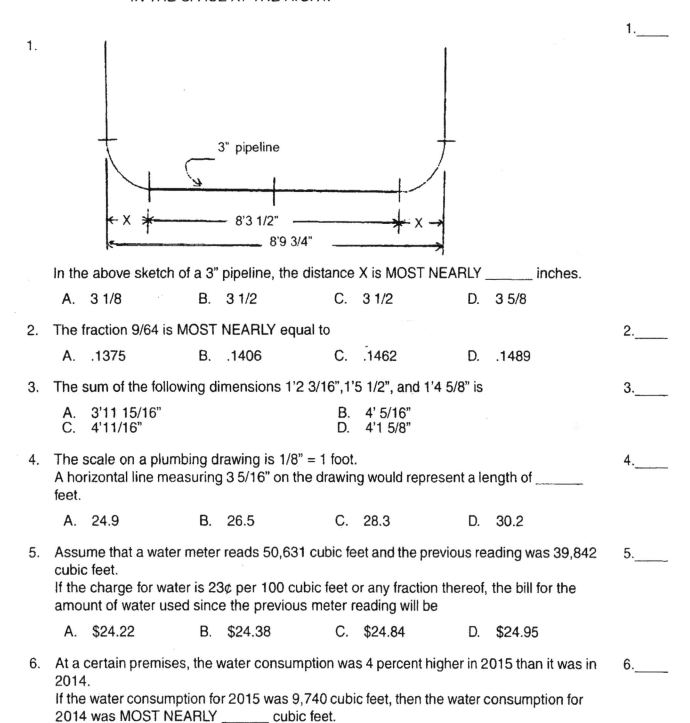

   In the above sketch of a 3" pipeline, the distance X is MOST NEARLY _____ inches.

   A. 3 1/8   B. 3 1/2   C. 3 1/2   D. 3 5/8

2. The fraction 9/64 is MOST NEARLY equal to

   A. .1375   B. .1406   C. .1462   D. .1489

3. The sum of the following dimensions 1'2 3/16", 1'5 1/2", and 1'4 5/8" is

   A. 3'11 15/16"   B. 4' 5/16"
   C. 4'11/16"   D. 4'1 5/8"

4. The scale on a plumbing drawing is 1/8" = 1 foot.
   A horizontal line measuring 3 5/16" on the drawing would represent a length of _____ feet.

   A. 24.9   B. 26.5   C. 28.3   D. 30.2

5. Assume that a water meter reads 50,631 cubic feet and the previous reading was 39,842 cubic feet.
   If the charge for water is 23¢ per 100 cubic feet or any fraction thereof, the bill for the amount of water used since the previous meter reading will be

   A. $24.22   B. $24.38   C. $24.84   D. $24.95

6. At a certain premises, the water consumption was 4 percent higher in 2015 than it was in 2014.
   If the water consumption for 2015 was 9,740 cubic feet, then the water consumption for 2014 was MOST NEARLY _____ cubic feet.

   A. 9,320   B. 9,350   C. 9,365   D. 9,390

7. A pump delivers water at a constant rate of 40 gallons per minute.
   If there are 7.5 gallons to a cubic foot of water, the time it will take to fill a tank 6 feet x 5 feet x 4 feet is MOST NEARLY _____ minutes.

   A. 15   B. 22.5   C. 28.5   D. 30

8. The total weight, in pounds, of three lengths of 3" cast-iron pipe 7'6" long, weighing 14.5 pounds per foot, and four lengths of 4" cast-iron pipe each 5'0" long, weighing 13.0 pounds per foot, is MOST NEARLY

   A. 540   B. 585   C. 600   D. 665

9. The water pressure at the bottom of a column of water 34 feet high is 14.7 lbs./sq.in.
   The water pressure in lbs./sq.in. at the bottom of the column of water 12 feet high is MOST NEARLY

   A. 3   B. 5   C. 7   D. 9

10. The number of cubic yards of earth that would be removed when digging a trench 8 feet wide x 9 feet deep x 63 feet long is

    A. 56   B. 168   C. 314   D. 504

11. On test, a meter registered one cubic foot for each 1 1/3 cubic feet of water that passed through it.
    If the meter had a reading of 1,200 cubic feet, we may conclude that the CORRECT amount should be _____ cubic feet.

    A. 800   B. 900   C. 1,500   D. 1,600

12. A water use meter reads 87,463 cubic feet.
    If the previous reading was 17,377 cubic feet and the rate charged is 15 cents per 100 cubic feet, the bill for water use during this period is about

    A. $45.00   B. $65.00   C. $85.00   D. $105.00

13. Under proper conditions, the one of the following groups of pipes that gives the same flow in gals/min as one 6" diameter pipe is (neglect friction) _____ pipes of _____ diameter each.

    A. 3; 3"   B. 4; 3"   C. 2; 4"   D. 3; 4"

14. A roof tank is used to furnish the domestic water supply to a ten story building. This tank has a capacity of 5,900 gallons. At 10:00 A.M. one morning, the tank is half full.
    If water is being used at the rate of 50 gals/min, the pump which is used to fill the tank has a rated capacity of 90 gals/min, the time it would take to fill the tank under these conditions is MOST NEARLY _____ hour(s), _____ minutes.

    A. 2; 8   B. 1; 14   C. 2; 32   D. 1; 2

15. The number of gallons of water contained in a cylindrical swimming pool 8 feet in diameter and filled to a depth of 3 feet 6 inches is MOST NEARLY (assume 7.5 gallons = 1 cubic foot)

    A. 30   B. 225   C. 1,320   D. 3,000

16. The charge for metered water is 52 1/2 cents per hundred cubic feet, with a minimum charge of $21 per annum. Of the following, the SMALLEST water usage in hundred cubic feet that would result in a charge GREATER than the minimum is

    A. 39   B. 40   C. 41   D. 42

17. The annual frontage rent on a one-story building 40 ft. in length is $735.00. For each additional story, $52.50 per annum is added to the frontage rent. For demolition, the charge for wetting down is 3/8 of the annual frontage charge.
    The charge for wetting down a building six stories in height, with a 40 ft. frontage, is MOST NEARLY

    A. $369   B. $371   C. $372   D. $374

18. If the drawing of a piping layout is made to a scale of 1/4" equals one foot, then a 7'9" length of piping would be represented by a scaled length on the drawing of APPROXIMATELY _____ inches.

    A. 2   B. 7 3/4   C. 23 1/4   D. 31

19. A plumbing sketch is drawn to a scale of eighth-size. A line measuring 3" on the sketch would be equivalent to _____ feet.

    A. 2   B. 6   C. 12   D. 24

20. If 500 feet of pipe weighs 800 lbs., the number of pounds that 120 feet will weigh is MOST NEARLY

    A. 190   B. 210   C. 230   D. 240

21. If a trench is excavated 3'0" wide by 5'6" deep and 50 feet long, the total number of cubic yards of earth removed is MOST NEARLY

    A. 30   B. 90   C. 150   D. 825

22. Assume that a plumber earns $86,500 per year.
    If eighteen percent of his pay is deducted for taxes and social security, his net weekly pay will be APPROXIMATELY

    A. $1,326   B. $1,365   C. $1,436   D. $1,457.50

23. Assume that a plumbing installation is made up of the following fixtures and groups of fixtures: 12 bathroom groups each containing one W.C., one lavatory, and one bathtub with shower; 12 bathroom groups each containing one W.C., one lavatory, one bathtub, and one shower stall; 24 combination kitchen fixtures; 4 floor drains; 6 slop sinks without flushing rim; and 2 shower stalls (or shower bath).
    The total number of fixtures for the above plumbing installation is MOST NEARLY

    A. 60   B. 95   C. 120   D. 210

24. A triangular opening in a wall forms a 30-60 degree right triangle.
    If the longest side measures 12'0", then the shortest side will measure

    A. 3'0"   B. 4'0"   C. 6'0"   D. 8'0"

25. You are directed to cut 4 pieces of pipe, one each of the following length: 2'6 1/4", 3'9 3/8", 4'7 5/8", and 5'8 7/8".
    The total length of these 4 pieces is

    A. 15'7 1/4"   B. 15'9 3/8"   C. 16'5 7/8"   D. 16'8 1/8"

25.____

KEY (CORRECT ANSWERS)

1. A
2. B
3. B
4. B
5. C

6. C
7. B
8. B
9. B
10. B

11. D
12. D
13. B
14. B
15. C

16. C
17. D
18. A
19. A
20. A

21. A
22. B
23. C
24. C
25. D

SOLUTIONS TO PROBLEMS

1. 8'3 1/2" + x + x = 8'9 3/4" Then, 2x = 6 1/4", so x = 3 1/8"

2. 9/64 = .140625 = .1406

3. 1'2 3/16" + 1'5 1/2" +1'4 5/8" = 3'11 21/16" = 4'5/16"

4. 3 5/16" ÷ 1/8" =53/16 x 8/1 = 26.5. Then, (26.5)(1 ft.) = 26.5 feet

5. 50,631 - 39,842 = 10,789; 10,789 ÷ 100 = 107.89
   Since the cost is .23 per 100 cubic feet or any fraction thereof, the cost will be
   (.23)(107) + .23 = $24.84

6. 9740 ÷ 1.04 = 9365 cu.ft.

7. 40 ÷ 7.5 = 5 1/3 cu.ft. of water per minute. The volume = (6)(5)(4) = 120 cu.ft. Thus, the number of minutes needed to fill the tank is 120 ÷ 5 1/3 = 22.5

8. 3" pipe: 3 x 7'6" = 22 1/2' x 14.5 lbs. = 326.25
   4" pipe: 4 x 5' = 20' x 13 lbs. = 260
   326.25 + 260 = 586.25 (most nearly 585)

9. Let x = pressure. Then, 34/12 = 14.7/x. So, 34x = 176.4
   Solving, x ≈ 5 lbs./sq.in.

10. (8)(9)(63) = 4536 cu.ft. Since 1 cu.yd. = 27 cu.ft., 4536 cu.ft. is equivalent to 168 cu.yds.

11. Let x = correct amount. Then, $\frac{1}{1200} = \frac{1\frac{1}{3}}{x}$. Solving, x = 1600

12. 87,463 - 17,377 = 70,086; and 70,086 ÷ 100 = 700.86 ≈ 700 Then, (700)(.15) = $105.00

13. Cross-sectional area of a 6" diameter pipe = (π)(3")^2 = 9π sq. in. Note that the combined cross-sectional areas of four 3" diameter pipes = (4)(π)(1.5")^2 = 9π sq. in.

14. 90 - 50 = 40 gals/min. Then, 2950 ÷ 40 = 73.75 min. ≈ 1 hr. 14 min.

15. Volume = (π)(4)^2(3 1/2) = 56π cu.ft. Then, (56π)(7.5) = 1320 gals.

16. For 4100 cu.ft., the charge of (.525)(41) = $21,525 > $21

17. Rent = $73,500 + (5)($52.50) = $997,50. For demolition, the charge = (3/8)($997.50) $374

18. (1/4")(7.75) = 2"

19. (3")(8) = 24" = 2 ft.

20. Let x = weight. Then, 500/800 = 120/x . Solving, x = 192 190 lbs.

21. (3')(5 1/2')(50') = 825 cu.ft. Then, 825 ÷ 27 ≈ 30 cu.yds.

22. Net pay = (.82)($86,500) = $70,930/yr. Weekly pay = $70,930 ÷ 52 ≈ $1365

23. (12x3) + (12x4) +24+4+6+2= 120

24. The shortest side = (1/2)(hypotenuse) = (1/2)(12') = 6'

25. 2'6 1/4" + 3'9 3/8" + 4'7 5/8" + 5'8 7/8 " = 14'30 17/8" = 16'8 1/8"

TEST 2

DIRECTIONS: Each question or incomplete statement is followed by several suggested answers or completions. Select the one that BEST answers the question or completes the statement. *PRINT THE LETTER OF THE CORRECT ANSWER IN THE SPACE AT THE RIGHT.*

1. The sum of the following pipe lengths, 15 5/8", 8 3/4", 30 5/16" and 20 1/2", is   1._____

   A. 77 1/8"   B. 76 3/16"   C. 75 3/16"   D. 74 5/16"

2. If the outside diameter of a pipe is 6 inches and the wall thickness is 1/2 inch, the inside area of this pipe, in square inches, is MOST NEARLY   2._____

   A. 15.7   B. 17.3   C. 19.6   D. 23.8

3. Three lengths of pipe 1'10", 3'2 1/2", and 5'7 1/2", respectively, are to be cut from a pipe 14'0" long.
   Allowing 1/8" for each pipe cut, the length of pipe remaining is   3._____

   A. 3'1 1/8"   B. 3'2 1/2"   C. 3'3 1/4"   D. 3'3 5/8"

4. According to the building code, the MAXIMUM permitted surface temperature of combustible construction materials located near heating equipment is 76.5°C. (°F=(°Cx9/5)+32)
   Maximum temperature Fahrenheit is MOST NEARLY   4._____

   A. 170° F   B. 195° F   C. 210° F   D. 220° F

5. A pump discharges 7.5 gals/minutes.
   In 2.5 hours the pump will discharge _____ gallons.   5._____

   A. 1125   B. 1875   C. 1950   D. 2200

6. A pipe with an outside diameter of 4" has a circumference of MOST NEARLY _____ inches.   6._____

   A. 8.05   B. 9.81   C. 12.57   D. 14.92

7. A piping sketch is drawn to a scale of 1/8" = 1 foot.
   A vertical steam line measuring 3 1/2" on the sketch would have an ACTUAL length of _____ feet.   7._____

   A. 16   B. 22   C. 24   D. 28

8. A pipe having an inside diameter of 3.48 inches and a wall thickness of .18 inches will have an outside diameter of _____ inches.   8._____

   A. 3.84   B. 3.64   C. 3.57   D. 3.51

9. A rectangular steel bar having a volume of 30 cubic inches, a width of 2 inches, and a height of 3 inches will have a length of _____ inches.   9._____

   A. 12   B. 10   C. 8   D. 5

10. A pipe weighs 20.4 pounds per foot of length.
    The total weight of eight pieces of this pipe with each piece 20 feet in length is MOST NEARLY _____ pounds.   10._____

    A. 460   B. 1,680   C. 2,420   D. 3,260

11. Assume that four pieces of pipe measuring 2'1 1/4", 4'2 3/4", 5'1 9/16", and 6'3 5/8", respectively, are cut with a saw from a pipe 20'0" long.
    Allowing 1/16" waste for each cut, the length of the remaining pipe is

    A. 2'1 9/16"   B. 2'2 9/16"   C. 2'4 13/16"   D. 2'8 9/16"

12. If one cubic inch of steel weighs 0.28 pounds, the weight, in pounds, of a steel bar 1/2" x 6" x 2'0" long is MOST NEARLY

    A. 11   B. 16   C. 20   D. 24

13. If the circumference of a circle is equal to 31.416 inches, then its diameter, in inches, is equal to MOST NEARLY

    A. 8   B. 9   C. 10   D. 13

14. Assume that a steam fitter's helper receives a salary of $171.36 a day for 250 days is considered a full work year. If taxes, social security, hospitalization, and pension deducted from his salary amounts to 16 percent of his gross pay, then his net yearly salary will be MOST NEARLY

    A. $31,788   B. $35,982   C. $41,982   D. $42,840

15. If the outside diameter of a pipe is 14 inches and the wall thickness is 1/2 inch, then the inside area of the pipe, in square inches, is MOST NEARLY

    A. 125   B. 133   C. 143   D. 154

16. A steam leak in a pipe line allows steam to escape at a rate of 50,000 pounds each month.
    Assuming that the cost of steam is $2.50 per 1,000 pounds, the TOTAL cost of wasted steam from this leak for a 12-month period would amount to

    A. $125   B. $300   C. $1,500   D. $3,000

17. If 250 feet of 4" pipe weighs 400 pounds, the weight of this pipe per linear foot is _____ pounds.

    A. 1.25   B. 1.50   C. 1.60   D. 1.75

18. A set of heating plan drawings is drawn to a scale of 1/4" = 1 foot.
    If a length of pipe measures 4 5/8" on the drawing, the ACTUAL length of the pipe, in feet, is

    A. 16.3   B. 16.8   C. 17.5   D. 18.5

19. The TOTAL length of four pieces of pipe whose lengths are 3'4 1/2", 2'1 5/16", 4'9 3/8", and 2'3 1/4", respectively, is

    A. 11'5 7/16"   B. 11'6 7/16"
    C. 12'5 7/16"   D. 12'6 7/16"

20. Assume that a pipe trench is 3 feet wide, 3 feet deep, and 300 feet long.
    If the unit cost of excavating the trench is $120 per cubic yard, the TOTAL cost of excavating the trench is

    A. $1,200   B. $12,000   C. $27,000   D. $36,000

21. The TOTAL length of four pieces of 1 1/2" galvanized steel pipe whose lengths are 7 ft. + 3 1/2 inches, 4 ft. + 2 1/4 inches, 6 ft. + 7 inches, and 8 ft. +5 1/8 inches is   21._____

    A. 26 feet + 5 7/8 inches   B. 25 ft. + 6 7/8 inches
    C. 25 feet + 4 1/4 inches   D. 25 ft. + 3 3/8 inches

22. A swimming pool is 25' wide by 75' long and has an average depth of 5'. 1 cubic foot contains 7.5 gallons of water. The capacity, when filled to the overflow, is _____ gallons.   22._____

    A. 9,375   B. 65,625   C. 69,005   D. 70,312

23. The sum of 3 1/4, 5 1/8, 2 1/2, and 3 3/8 is   23._____

    A. 14   B. 14 1/8   C. 14 1/4   D. 14 3/8

24. Assume that it takes 6 men 8 days to do a particular job. If you have only 4 men available to do this job and they all work at the same speed, then the number of days it would take to complete the job would be   24._____

    A. 11   B. 12   C. 13   D. 14

25. The total length of four pieces of 2" O.D. pipe, whose lengths are 7'3 1/2", 4'2 3/16", 5'7 5/16", and 8'5 7/8", respectively, is MOST NEARLY   25._____

    A. 24'6 3/4"   B. 24'7 15/16"
    C. 25'5 13/16"   D. 25'6 7/8"

KEY (CORRECT ANSWERS)

1. C		11. B	
2. C		12. C	
3. D		13. C	
4. A		14. B	
5. A		15. B	
6. C		16. C	
7. D		17. C	
8. A		18. D	
9. D		19. D	
10. D		20. B	

21. A
22. D
23. C
24. B
25. D

SOLUTIONS TO PROBLEMS

1. 15 5/8" + 8 3/4" + 30 5/16" + 20 1/2" = 73 35/16" = 75 3/16"

2. Inside diameter = 6" - 1/2" - 1/2" = 5". Area = $(\pi)(5/2")^2 \approx$ 19.6 sq. in.

3. Pipe remaining = 14' - 1'10" - 3'2 1/2" - 5'7 1/2" - (3)(1/8") = 3'3 5/8"

4. 76.5 x 9/5 = 137.7 + 32 = 169.7

5. 7.5 x 150 = 1125

6. Radius = 2" Circumference = $(2\pi)(2") \approx$ 12.57"

7. 3 1/2" 1/8" = (7/2)(8/1) = 28 Then, (28)(1 ft.) = 28 feet

8. Outside diameter = 3.48" + .18" + .18" = 3.84"

9. 30 = (2)(3)(length). So, length = 5"

10. Total weight = (20.4)(8)(20) $\approx$ 3260 lbs.

11. 20' - 2'1 1/4" - 4'2 3/4" - 5'1 9/16" - 6'3 5/8" - (4)(1/16") = 2'2 9/16"

12. Weight = (.28)(1/2")(6")(24") = 20.16 $\approx$ 20 lbs.

13. Diameter = 31.416" $\div \pi \approx$ 10"

14. His net pay for 250 days = (.84)($171.36)(250) = $35,985.60 $\approx$ $35,928 (from answer key)

15. Inside diameter = 14" - 1/2" - 1/2" = 13". Area = $(\pi)(13/2")^2 \approx$ 133 sq.in

16. (50,000 lbs.)(12) = 600,000 lbs. per year. The cost would be ($2.50)(600) = $1500

17. 400 $\div$ 250 = 1.60 pounds per linear foot

18. 4 5/8" $\div$ 1/4" = 37/8 . 4/1 = 18.5 Then, (18.5)(1 ft.) = 18.5 feet

19. 3'4 1/2" + 2'1 5/16" + 4'9 3/8" + 2'3 1/4" = 11'17 23/16" = 12'6 7/16"

20. (3')(3')(300') = 2700 cu.ft., which is 2700 $\div$ 27 = 100 cu.yds. Total cost = ($120)(100) = $12,000

21. 7'3 1/2" + 4'2 1/4" + 6'7" + 8'5 1/8" = 25'17 7/8" = 26'5 7/8"

22. (25)(75)(5) = 9375 cu.ft. Then, (9375)(7.5) $\approx$ 70,312 gals.

23. 3 1/4 + 5 1/8 + 2 1/2 + 3 3/8 = 13 10/8 = 14 1/4

24. (6)(8) = 48 man-days. Then, 48 $\div$ 4 = 12 days

25. 7'3 1/2" + 4'2 3/16" + 5'7 5/16" + 8'5 7/8" = 24'17 30/16" = 25'6 7/8"

TEST 3

DIRECTIONS: Each question or incomplete statement is followed by several suggested answers or completions. Select the one that BEST answers the question or completes the statement. *PRINT THE LETTER OF THE CORRECT ANSWER IN THE SPACE AT THE RIGHT.*

1. The time required to pump 2,500 gallons of water out of a sump at the rate of 12 1/2 gallons per minutes would be _____ hour(s) _____ minutes.   1.____

   A. 1; 40   B. 2; 30   C. 3; 20   D. 6; 40

2. Copper tubing which has an inside diameter of 1 1/16" and a wall thickness of .095" has an outside diameter which is MOST NEARLY _____ inches.   2.____

   A. 1 5/32   B. 1 3/16   C. 1 7/32   D. 1 1/4

3. Assume that 90 gallons per minute flow through a certain 3-inch pipe which is tapped into a street main.   3.____
   The amount of water which would flow through a 1-inch pipe tapped into the same street main is MOST NEARLY _____ gpm.

   A. 90   B. 45   C. 30   D. 10

4. The weight of a 6 foot length of 8-inch pipe which weighs 24.70 pounds per foot is _____ lbs.   4.____

   A. 148.2   B. 176.8   C. 197.6   D. 212.4

5. If a 4-inch pipe is directly coupled to a 2-inch pipe and 16 gallons per minute are flowing through the 4-inch pipe, then the flow through the 2-inch pipe will be _____ gallons per minute.   5.____

   A. 4   B. 8   C. 16   D. 32

6. If the water pressure at the bottom of a column of water 34 feet high is 14.7 pounds per square inch, the water pressure at the bottom of a column of water 18 feet high is MOST NEARLY _____ pounds per square inch.   6.____

   A. 8.0   B. 7.8   C. 7.6   D. 7.4

7. If there are 7 1/2 gallons in a cubic foot of water and if water flows from a hose at a constant rate of 4 gallons per minute, the time it should take to COMPLETELY fill a tank of 1,600 cubic feet capacity with water from that hose is _____ hours.   7.____

   A. 300   B. 150   C. 100   D. 50

8. Each of a group of fifteen water meter readers read an average of 62 water meters a day in a certain 5-day work week. A total of 5,115 meters are read by this group the following week.   8.____
   The TOTAL number of meters read in the second week as compared to the first week shows a

   A. 10% increase   B. 15% increase
   C. 20% increase   D. 5% decrease

9. A certain water consumer used 5% more water in 1994 than he did in 1993. If his water consumption for 1994 was 8,375 cubic feet, the amount of water he consumed in 1993 was MOST NEARLY _____ cubic feet.

   A. 9,014   B. 8,816   C. 7,976   D. 6,776

10. Assume that a water meter reads 40,175 cubic feet and that the previous reading was 29,186 cubic feet.
    If the charge for water is 92 cents per 100 cubic feet or any fraction thereof, the bill for the amount of water used since the previous meter reading should be

    A. $100.28   B. $101.04   C. $101.08   D. $101.20

11. A leaking faucet caused a loss of 216 cubic feet of water in a 30-day month. If there are 7.5 gallons in a cubic foot of water, then the AVERAGE loss of water per hour for that month was _____ gallons.

    A. 2 1/4   B. 2 1/8   C. 2   D. 1 3/4

12. The fraction which is equal to .375 is

    A. 3/16   B. 5/32   C. 3/8   D. 5/12

13. A square backyard swimming pool, each side of which is 10 feet long, is filled to a depth of 3 1/2 feet.
    If there are 7 1/2 gallons in a cubic foot of water, the number of gallons of water in the pool is MOST NEARLY _____ gallons.

    A. 46.7   B. 100   C. 2,625   D. 3,500

14. When 1 5/8, 3 3/4, 6 1/3, and 9 1/2 are added, the resulting sum is

    A. 21 1/8   B. 21 1/6   C. 21 5/24   D. 21 1/4

15. When 946 1/2 is subtracted from 1,035 1/4, the result is

    A. 87 1/4   B. 87 3/4   C. 88 1/4   D. 88 3/4

16. When 39 is multiplied by 697, the result is

    A. 8,364   B. 26,283   C. 27,183   D. 28,003

17. When 16.074 is divided by .045, the result is

    A. 3.6   B. 35.7   C. 357.2   D. 3,572

18. To dig a trench 3'0" wide, 50'0" long, and 5'6" deep, the total number of cubic yards of earth to be removed is MOST NEARLY

    A. 30   B. 90   C. 140   D. 825

19. The TOTAL length of four pieces of 2" pipe, whose lengths are 7'3 1/2", 4'2 3/16", 5'7 5/16", and 8'5 7/8", respectively, is

    A. 24'6 3/4"   B. 24'7 15/16"
    C. 25'5 13/16"   D. 25'6 7/8"

20. A hot water line made of copper has a straight horizontal run of 150 feet and, when installed, is at a temperature of 45° F. In use, its temperature rises to 190° F. If the coefficient of expansion for copper is 0.0000095" per foot per degree F, the TOTAL expansion, in inches, in the run of pipe is given by the product of 150 multiplied by 0.0000095 by

    A. 145
    B. 145 x 12
    C. 145 divided by 12
    D. 145 x 12 x 12

21. A water storage tank measures 5' long, 4' wide, and 6' deep and is filled to the 5 1/2' mark with water.
    If one cubic foot of water weighs 62 pounds, the number of pounds of water required to COMPLETELY fill the tank is

    A. 7,440   B. 6,200   C. 1,240   D. 620

22. Assume that a pipe worker earns $83,125.00 per year.
    If seventeen percent of his pay is deducted for taxes, social security, and pension, his net weekly pay will be APPROXIMATELY

    A. $1598.50   B. $1504.00   C. $1453.00   D. $1325.00

23. If eighteen feet of 4" cast iron pipe weighs approximately 390 pounds, the weight of this pipe per lineal foot will be MOST NEARLY _____ lbs.

    A. 19   B. 22   C. 23   D. 25

24. If it takes 3 men 11 days to dig a trench, the number of days it will take 5 men to dig the same trench, assuming all work is done at the same rate of speed, is MOST NEARLY

    A. 6 1/2   B. 7 3/4   C. 8 1/4   D. 8 3/4

25. If a trench is dug 6'0" deep, 2'6" wide, and 8'0" long, the area of the opening, in square feet, is MOST NEARLY

    A. 48   B. 32   C. 20   D. 15

KEY (CORRECT ANSWERS)

1. C
2. D
3. D
4. A
5. B

6. B
7. D
8. A
9. C
10. D

11. A
12. C
13. C
14. C
15. D

16. C
17. C
18. A
19. D
20. A

21. D
22. D
23. B
24. A
25. C

SOLUTIONS TO PROBLEMS

1. 2500 ÷ 12 1/2 = 200 min. = 3 hrs. 20 min.

2. 1 1/16" + .095" + .095" = 1.0625 + .095 + .095 = 1.2525" ≈ 1 1/4"

3. Cross-sectional areas for a 3-inch pipe and a 1-inch pipe are $(\pi)(1.5)^2$ and $(\pi)(.5)^2$ = 2.25π and $.25\pi$, respectively. Let x = amount of water flowing through the 1-inch pipe. Then, $\frac{90}{x} = \frac{2.25\pi}{.25\pi}$. Solving, x = 10 gals/min

4. (24.70)(6) = 148.2 lbs.

5. $\frac{4" \text{ pipe}}{16 \text{ gallons}} = \frac{2" \text{ pipe}}{x \text{ gallons}}$, 4x = 32, x = 8

6. Let x = pressure. Then, 34/18 = 14.7/x. Solving, x ≈ 7.8

7. (1600)(7.5) = 12,000 gallons. Then, 12,000 ÷ 4 = 3000 min. = 50 hours

8. (15)(62)(5) = 4650. Then, (5115-4650)/4650 = 10% increase

9. 8375 ÷ 1.05 ≈ 7976 cu.ft.

10. 40,175 - 29,186 = 10,989 cu.ft. Then, 10,989 100 = 109.89. Since .92 is charged for each 100 cu.ft. or fraction thereof, total cost = (.92)(110) = $101.20

11. (216)(7.5) = 1620 gallons. In 30 days, there are 720 hours. Thus, the average water loss per hour = 1620 ÷ 720 = 2 1/4 gallons.

12. .375 = 375/1000 = 3/8

13. Volume = (10)(10)(3 1/2) = 350 cu.ft. Then, (350)(7 1/2) = 2625 gallons

14. 1 5/8 + 3 3/4 + 6 1/3 + 9 1/2 = 19 53/24 = 21 5/24

15. 1035 1/4 - 946 1/2 = 88 3/4

16. (39)(697) = 27,183

17. 16.074 .045 = 357.2

18. (3')(50')(5 1/2') = 825 cu.ft. ≈ 30 cu.yds., since 1 cu.yd. = 27 cu.ft.

19. 7'3 1/2" + 4'2 3/16" + 5'7 5/16" + 8'5 7/8" = 24'17 30/16" = 25'6 7/8"

20. Total expansion = (150)(.0000095)(145)

21. Number of pounds needed = (5) (4)(6-5 1/2)(62) = 620

22. Net annual pay = ($83,125)(.83) ≈ $69000. Then, the net weekly pay = $69000 ÷ 52 ≈ $1325 (actually about $1327)

23. 390 lbs. ÷ 18 = 21.6 lbs. per linear foot

24. (3)(11) = 33 man-days. Then, 33 ÷ 5 = 6.6 ≈ 6 1/2 days

25. Area = (8')(2 1/2') = 20 sq.ft.

NAME AND NUMBER CHECKING

EXAMINATION SECTION
TEST 1

DIRECTIONS: Questions 1 through 17 consist of sets of names and addresses. In each question, the name and address in Column II should be an exact copy of the name and address in Column I.

If there is:
a mistake only in the name, mark your answer A;
a mistake only in the address, mark your answer B;
a mistake in both name and address, mark your answer C;
NO mistake in either name or address, mark your answer D.

SAMPLE QUESTION

Column I

Christina Magnusson
288 Greene Street
New York, N.Y. 10003

Column II

Christina Magnusson
288 Greene Street
New York, N.Y. 10013

Since there is a mistake only in the address (the zip code should be 10003 instead of 10013), the answer to the sample question is B.

COLUMN I

1. Ms. Joan Kelly
   313 Franklin Ave.
   Brooklyn, N.Y. 11202

2. Mrs. Eileen Engel
   47-24 86 Road
   Queens, N.Y. 11122

3. Marcia Michaels
   213 E. 81 St.
   New York, N.Y. 10012

4. Rev. Edward J. Smyth
   1401 Brandeis Street
   San Francisco, Calif. 96201

5. Alicia Rodriguez
   24-68 81 St.
   Elmhurst, N.Y. 11122

6. Ernest Eisemann
   21 Columbia St.
   New York, N.Y. 10007

COLUMN II

1. Ms. Joan Kielly
   318 Franklin Ave.
   Brooklyn, N.Y. 11202

2. Mrs. Ellen Engel
   47-24 86 Road
   Queens, N.Y. 11122

3. Marcia Michaels
   213 E. 81 St.
   New York, N.Y. 10012

4. Rev. Edward J. Smyth
   1401 Brandies Street
   San Francisco, Calif. 96201

5. Alicia Rodriguez
   2468 81 St.
   Elmhurst, N.Y. 11122

6. Ernest Eisermann
   21 Columbia St.
   New York, N.Y. 10007

1.____
2.____
3.____
4.____
5.____
6.____

Column I	COLUMN II	
7. Mr. & Mrs. George Petersson 87-11 91st Avenue Woodhaven, N.Y. 11421	Mr. & Mrs. George Peterson 87-11 91st Avenue Woodhaven, N.Y. 11421	7.____
8. Mr. Ivan Klebnikov 1848 Newkirk Avenue Brooklyn, N.Y. 11226	Mr. Ivan Klebikov 1848 Newkirk Avenue Brooklyn, N.Y. 11622	8.____
9. Samuel Rothfleisch 71 Pine Street New York, N.Y. 10005	Samuel Rothfleisch 71 Pine Street New York, N.Y. 10005	9.____
10. Mrs. Isabel Tonnessen 198 East 185th Street Bronx, N.Y. 10458	Mrs. Isabel Tonnessen 189 East 185th Street Bronx, N.Y. 10458	10.____
11. Esteban Perez 173 Eighth Street Staten Island, N.Y. 10306	Estaban Perez 173 Eighth Street Staten Island, N.Y. 10306	11.____
12. Esta Wong 141 West 68 St. New York, N.Y. 10023	Esta Wang 141 West 68 St. New York, N.Y. 10023	12.____
13. Dr. Alberto Grosso 3475 12th Avenue Brooklyn, N.Y. 11218	Dr. Alberto Grosso 3475 12th Avenue Brooklyn, N.Y. 11218	13.____
14. Mrs. Ruth Bortlas 482 Theresa Ct. Far Rockaway, N.Y. 11691	Ms. Ruth Bortlas 482 Theresa Ct. Far Rockaway, N.Y. 11169	14.____
15. Mr. & Mrs. Howard Fox 2301 Sedgwick Ave. Bronx, N.Y. 10468	Mr. & Mrs. Howard Fox 231 Sedgwick Ave. Bronx, N.Y. 10468	15.____
16. Miss Marjorie Black 223 East 23 Street New York, N.Y. 10010	Miss Margorie Black 223 East 23 Street New York, N.Y. 10010	16.____
17. Michelle Herman 806 Valley Rd. Old Tappan, N.J. 07675	Michelle Hermann 806 Valley Dr. Old Tappan, N.J. 07675	17.____

KEY (CORRECT ANSWERS)

1. C
2. A
3. D
4. B
5. B

6. A
7. A
8. C
9. D
10. B

11. A
12. A
13. D
14. C
15. B
16. A
17. C

TEST 2

DIRECTIONS: Questions 1 through 15 are to be answered SOLELY on the instructions given below. *PRINT THE LETTER OF THE CORRECT ANSWER IN THE SPACE AT THE RIGHT.*

INSTRUCTIONS:

In each of the following questions, the 3-line name and address in Column I is the master-list entry, and the 3-line entry in Column 2 is the information to be checked against the master list. If there is one line that does not match, mark your answer A; if there are two lines that do not match, mark your answer B; if all three lines do not match, mark your answer C; if the lines all match exactly, mark your answer D.

SAMPLE QUESTION

Column I
Mark L. Field
11-09 Prince Park Blvd.
Bronx, N.Y. 11402

Column II
Mark L. Field
11-99 Prince Park Way
Bronx, N.Y. 11401

The first lines in each column match exactly. The second lines do not match since 11-<u>09</u> does not match 11-<u>99</u>; and <u>Blvd.</u> does not match <u>Way</u>. The third lines do not match either since 1140<u>2</u> does not match 1140<u>1</u>. Therefore, there are two lines that do not match, and the CORRECT answer is B.

COLUMN I

1. Jerome A. Jackson
   1243 14th Avenue
   New York, N.Y. 10023

2. Sophie Strachtheim
   33-28 Connecticut Ave.
   Far Rockaway, N.Y. 11697

3. Elisabeth N.T. Gorrell
   256 Exchange St.
   New York, N.Y. 10013

4. Maria J. Gonzalez
   7516 E. Sheepshead Rd.
   Brooklyn, N.Y. 11240

5. Leslie B. Brautenweiler
   21 57A Seiler Terr.
   Flushing, N.Y. 11367

6. Rigoberto J. Peredes
   157 Twin Towers, #18F
   Tottenville, S.I., N.Y.

COLUMN II

1. Jerome A. Johnson
   1234 14th Avenue
   New York, N.Y. 10023

2. Sophie Strachtheim
   33-28 Connecticut Ave.
   Far Rockaway, N.Y. 11697

3. Elizabeth N.T. Gorrell
   256 Exchange St.
   New York, N.Y. 10013

4. Maria J. Gonzalez
   7516 N. Shepshead Rd.
   Brooklyn, N.Y. 11240

5. Leslie B. Brautenwieler
   21-75A Seiler Terr.
   Flushing, N.J. 11367

6. Rigoberto J. Peredes
   157 Twin Towers, #18F
   Tottenville, S.I., N.Y.

1._____

2._____

3._____

4._____

5._____

6._____

COLUMN I

7. Pietro F. Albino
   P.O. Box 7548
   Floral Park, N.Y. 11005

8. Joanne Zimmermann
   Bldg. SW, Room 314
   532-4601

9. Carlyle Whetstone
   Payroll Div.-A, Room 212A
   262-5000, ext. 471

10. Kenneth Chiang
    Legal Council, Room 9745
    (201) 416-9100, ext. 17

11. Ethel Koenig
    Personnel Services Division,
    Room 433; 635-7572

12. Joyce Ehrhardt
    Office of the Administrator,
    Room W56; 387-8706

13. Ruth Lang
    EAM Bldg., Room C101
    625-2000, ext. 765

14. Anne Marie Ionozzi
    Investigations, Room 827
    576-4000, ext. 832

15. Willard Jameson
    Fm C Bldg., Room 687
    454-3010

COLUMN II

Pietro F. Albina
P.O. Box 7458
Floral Park, N.Y. 11005

Joanne Zimmermann
Bldg. SW, Room 314
532-4601

Caryle Whetstone
Payroll Div.-A, Room 212A
262-5000, ext. 417

Kenneth Chiang
Legal Counsel, Room 9745
(201) 416-9100, ext. 17

Ethel Hoenig
Personal Services Division,
Room 433; 635-7527

Joyce Ehrhart
Office of the Administrator,
Room W56; 387-7806

Ruth Lang
EAM Bldg., Room C110
625-2000, ext. 765

Anna Marie Ionozzi
Investigation, Room 827
566-4000, ext. 832

Willard Jamieson
Fm C Bldg., Room 687
454-3010

7. ____
8. ____
9. ____
10. ____
11. ____
12. ____
13. ____
14. ____
15. ____

KEY (CORRECT ANSWERS)

1. B
2. D
3. A
4. A
5. C

6. D
7. B
8. D
9. B
10. A

11. C
12. B
13. A
14. C
15. A

TEST 3

DIRECTIONS: Questions 1 through 10 are to be answered on the basis of the following instructions. *PRINT THE LETTER OF THE CORRECT ANSWER IN THE SPACE AT THE RIGHT.*

INSTRUCTIONS:

For each such set of names, addresses, and numbers listed in Columns I and II, select your answer from the following options:
- A. The names in Columns I and II are different.
- B. The addresses in Columns I and II are different.
- C. The numbers in Columns I and II are different.
- D. The names, addresses, and numbers in Columns I and II are identical.

	COLUMN I	COLUMN II	
1.	Francis Jones 62 Stately Avenue 96-12446	Francis Jones 62 Stately Avenue 96-21446	1.____
2.	Julio Montez 19 Ponderosa Road 56-73161	Julio Montez 19 Ponderosa Road 56-71361	2.____
3.	Mary Mitchell 2314 Melbourne Drive 68-92172	Mary Mitchell 2314 Melbourne Drive 68-92172	3.____
4.	Harry Patterson 25 Dunne Street 14-33430	Harry Patterson 25 Dunne Street 14-34330	4.____
5.	Patrick Murphy 171 West Hosmer Street 93-81214	Patrick Murphy 171 West Hosmer Street 93-18214	5.____
6.	August Schultz 816 St. Clair Avenue 53-40149	August Schultz 816 St. Claire Avenue 53-40149	6.____
7.	George Taft 72 Runnymede Street 47-04033	George Taft 72 Runnymede Street 47-04023	7.____
8.	Angus Henderson 1418 Madison Street 81-76375	Angus Henderson 1418 Madison Street 81-76375	8.____
9.	Carolyn Mazur 12 Riverview Road 38-99615	Carolyn Mazur 12 Rivervane ftoad 38-99615	9.____

COLUMN I	COLUMN II	
10. Adele Russell 1725 Lansing Lane 72-91962	Adela Russell 1725 Lansing Lane 72-91962	10.____

KEY (CORRECT ANSWERS)

1. C   6. B
2. C   7. C
3. D   8. D
4. C   9. B
5. C   10. A

TEST 4

DIRECTIONS: Questions 1 through 20 test how good you are at catching mistakes in typing or printing. In each question, the name and address in Column II should be an exact copy of the name and address in Column I. Mark your answer

    A. if there is no mistake in either name or address;
    B. if there is a mistake in both name and address;
    C. if there is a mistake only in the name;
    D. if there is a mistake only in the address.

PRINT THE LETTER OF THE CORRECT ANSWER IN THE SPACE AT THE RIGHT.

COLUMN I   COLUMN II

1. Milos Yanocek
   33-60 14 Street
   Long Island City, N.Y. 11011

   Milos Yanocek
   33-60 14 Street
   Long Island City, N.Y. 11001

   1.____

2. Alphonse Sabattelo
   24 Minnetta Lane
   New York, N.Y. 10006

   Alphonse Sabbattelo
   24 Minetta Lane
   New York, N.Y. 10006

   2.____

3. Helen Steam
   5 Metropolitan Oval
   Bronx, N.Y. 10462

   Helene Stearn
   5 Metropolitan Oval
   Bronx, N.Y. 10462

   3.____

4. Jacob Weisman
   231 Francis Lewis Boulevard
   Forest Hills, N.Y. 11325

   Jacob Weisman
   231 Francis Lewis Boulevard
   Forest Hills, N.Y. 11325

   4.____

5. Riccardo Fuente
   134 West 83 Street
   New York, N.Y. 10024

   Riccardo Fuentes
   134 West 88 Street
   New York, N.Y. 10024

   5.____

6. Dennis Lauber
   52 Avenue D
   Brooklyn, N.Y. 11216

   Dennis Lauder
   52 Avenue D
   Brooklyn, N.Y. 11216

   6.____

7. Paul Cutter
   195 Galloway Avenue
   Staten Island, N.Y. 10356

   Paul Cutter
   175 Galloway Avenue
   Staten Island, N.Y. 10365

   7.____

8. Sean Donnelly
   45-58 41 Avenue
   Woodside, N.Y. 11168

   Sean Donnelly
   45-58 41 Avenue
   Woodside, N.Y. 11168

   8.____

9. Clyde Willot
   1483 Rockaway Avenue
   Brooklyn, N.Y. 11238

   Clyde Willat
   1483 Rockaway Avenue
   Brooklyn, N.Y. 11238

   9.____

COLUMN I	COLUMN II	
10. Michael Stanakis 419 Sheriden Avenue Staten Island, N.Y. 10363	Michael Stanakis 419 Sheraden Avenue Staten Island, N.Y. 10363	10._____
11. Joseph DiSilva 63-84 Saunders Road Rego Park, N.Y. 11431	Joseph Disilva 64-83 Saunders Road Rego Park, N.Y. 11431	11._____
12. Linda Polansky 2225 Fenton Avenue Bronx, N.Y. 10464	Linda Polansky 2255 Fenton Avenue Bronx, N.Y. 10464	12._____
13. Alfred Klein 260 Hillside Terrace Staten Island, N.Y. 15545	Alfred Klein 260 Hillside Terrace Staten Island, N.Y. 15545	13._____
14. William McDonnell 504 E. 55 Street New York, N.Y. 10103	William McConnell 504 E. 55 Street New York, N.Y. 10108	14._____
15. Angela Cipolla 41-11 Parson Avenue Flushing, N.Y. 11446	Angela Cipola 41-11 Parsons Avenue Flushing, N.Y. 11446	15._____
16. Julie Sheridan 1212 Ocean Avenue Brooklyn, N.Y. 11237	Julia Sheridan 1212 Ocean Avenue Brooklyn, N.Y. 11237	16._____
17. Arturo Rodriguez 2156 Cruger Avenue Bronx, N.Y. 10446	Arturo Rodrigues 2156 Cruger Avenue Bronx, N.Y. 10446	17._____
18. Helen McCabe 2044 East 19 Street Brooklyn, N.Y. 11204	Helen McCabe 2040 East 19 Street Brooklyn,. N.Y. 11204	18._____
19. Charles Martin 526 West 160 Street New York, N.Y. 10022	Charles Martin 526 West 160 Street New York, N.Y. 10022	19._____
20. Morris Rabinowitz 31 Avenue M Brooklyn, N.Y. 11216	Morris Rabinowitz 31 Avenue N Brooklyn, N.Y. 11216	20._____

KEY (CORRECT ANSWERS)

1. D
2. B
3. C
4. A
5. B

6. C
7. D
8. A
9. B
10. D

11. B
12. D
13. A
14. B
15. B

16. C
17. C
18. D
19. A
20. D

TEST 5

DIRECTIONS: In copying the addresses below from Column A to the same line in Column B, an Agent-in-Training made some errors. For Questions 1 through 5, if you find that the Agent made an error in

      only one line, mark your answer A;
      only two lines, mark your answer B;
      only three lines, mark your answer C;
      all four lines, mark your answer D.

EXAMPLE

Column A	Column B
24 Third Avenue	24 Third Avenue
5 Lincoln Road	5 Lincoln Street
50 Central Park West	6 Central Park West
37-21 Queens Boulevard	21-37 Queens Boulevard

Since errors were made on only three lines, namely the second, third, and fourth, the CORRECT answer is C.
PRINT THE LETTER OF THE CORRECT ANSWER IN THE SPACE AT THE RIGHT.

	Column A	Column B	
1.	57-22 Springfield Boulevard 94 Gun Hill Road 8 New Dorp Lane 36 Bedford Avenue	75-22 Springfield Boulevard 94 Gun Hill Avenue 8 New Drop Lane 36 Bedford Avenue	1.____
2.	538 Castle Hill Avenue 54-15 Beach Channel Drive 21 Ralph Avenue 162 Madison Avenue	538 Castle Hill Avenue 54-15 Beach Channel Drive 21 Ralph Avenue 162 Morrison Avenue	2.____
3.	49 Thomas Street 27-21 Northern Blvd. 86 125th Street 872 Atlantic Ave.	49 Thomas Street 21-27 Northern Blvd. 86 125th Street 872 Baltic Ave.	3.____
4.	261-17 Horace Harding Expwy. 191 Fordham Road 6 Victory Blvd. 552 Oceanic Ave.	261-17 Horace Harding Pkwy. 191 Fordham Road 6 Victoria Blvd. 552 Ocean Ave.	4.____
5.	90-05 38th Avenue 19 Central Park West 9281 Avenue X 22 West Farms Square	90-05 36th Avenue 19 Central Park East 9281 Avenue X 22 West Farms Square	5.____

KEY (CORRECT ANSWERS)

1. C
2. A
3. B
4. C
5. B

TEST 6

Questions 1-10.

DIRECTIONS: For Questions 1 through 10, choose the letter in Column II next to the number which EXACTLY matches the number in Column I. *PRINT THE LETTER OF THE CORRECT ANSWER IN THE SPACE AT THE RIGHT.*

	COLUMN I		COLUMN II	
1.	14235	A. B. C. D.	13254 12435 13245 14235	1._____
2.	70698	A. B. C. D.	90768 60978 70698 70968	2._____
3.	11698	A. B. C. D.	11689 11986 11968 11698	3._____
4.	50497	A. B. C. D.	50947 50497 50749 54097	4._____
5.	69635	A. B. C. D.	60653 69630 69365 69635	5._____
6.	1201022011	A. B. C. D.	1201022011 1201020211 1202012011 1021202011	6._____
7.	3893981389	A. B. C. D.	3893891389 3983981389 3983891389 3893981389	7._____
8.	4765476589	A. B. C. D.	4765476598 4765476588 4765476589 4765746589	8._____

COLUMN I	COLUMN II	
9. 8679678938	A. 8679687938 B. 8679678938 C. 8697678938 D. 8678678938	9._____
10. 6834836932	A. 6834386932 B. 6834836923 C. 6843836932 D. 6834836932	10._____

Questions 11-15.

DIRECTIONS: For Questions 11 through 15, determine how many of the symbols in Column Z are exactly the same as the symbol in Column Y.
If none is exactly the same, answer A;
if only one symbol is exactly the same, answer B;
if two symbols are exactly the same, answer C;
if three symbols are exactly the same, answer D.

COLUMN Y	COLUMN Z	
11. A123B1266	A123B1366 A123B1266 A133B1366 A123B1266	11._____
12. CC28D3377	CD22D3377 CC38D3377 CC28C3377 CC28D2277	12._____
13. M21AB201X	M12AB201X M21AB201X M21AB201Y M21BA201X	13._____
14. PA383Y744	AP383Y744 PA338Y744 PA388Y744 PA383Y774	14._____
15. PB2Y8893	PB2Y8893 PB2Y8893 PB3Y8898 PB2Y8893	15._____

KEY (CORRECT ANSWERS)

1. D
2. C
3. D
4. B
5. D

6. A
7. D
8. C
9. B
10. D

11. C
12. A
13. B
14. A
15. D

GLOSSARY

Acre-foot. A unit quantity of water; an amount which would cover 1 acre to a depth of 1 foot; consists of 326,000 gallons.

Alum. A chemical substance that is gelatinous when wet, usually potassium aluminum sulfate, used in water treatment plants for settling out small particles of foreign matter.

Consumptive use. Use of water resulting in a large proportion of loss to the atmosphere by evapotranspiration. Irrigation is consumptive use.

Crumb. A unit or particle of soil composed of many small grains sticking together.

Cubic feet per second (cfs). A measure of discharge; the amount of water passing a given point, expressed as number of cubic feet in each second.

Discharge. Outflow; the flow of a stream, canal, or aquifer. One may also speak of the discharge of a canal or stream into a lake, river, or an ocean.

Divide, drainage divide (sometimes called *watershed*). The boundary between one drainage basin and another.

Domestic use. Water use in homes and on lawns, including use for laundry, washing cars, cooling, and swimming pools.

Draw. A tributary valley or coulee, that usually discharges water only after a rainstorm.

Evaporation. The process by which water is changed from a liquid to a gas or vapor.

Evapotranspiration. Water withdrawn from soil by evaporation and plant transpiration. This water is transmitted to the atmosphere as vapor.

Flood. Any relatively high stream flow overtopping the natural or artificial banks in any reach of a stream.

Flood plain. The lowland that borders a river, usually dry but subject to flooding when the stream overflows its banks.

Food chain. The dependence of one type of life on another, each in turn eating or absorbing the next organism in the chain. Grass is eaten by cow; cow is eaten by man. This food chain involves grass, cow, and man.

Head race. The pipe or chute by which water falls downward into the turbine of a power plant.

Humus. Organic matter in or on a soil; composed of partly or fully decomposed bits of plant tissue derived from plants on or in the soil, or from animal manure.

Hydrology. The science of the behavior of water in the atmosphere, on surface of the earth, and underground.

Infiltration. The flow of a fluid into a substance through pores or small openings. The common use of the word is to denote the flow of water into soil material.

Leaching. The removal in solution of the more soluble minerals by percolating waters.

Nonconsumptive use. Uses of water in which but a small part of the water is lost to the atmosphere by evapotranspiration or by being combined with a manufactured product. Nonconsumptive uses return to the stream or the ground approximately the same amount as diverted or used.

Permeability. The property of soil or rock to pass water through it. This depends not only on the volume of the openings and pores, but also on how these openings are connected one to another.

Reaction turbine. A type of water wheel in which water turns the blades of a rotor, which then drives an electrical generator or other machine.

Salts. Dissolved chemical substances in water; table salt (sodium chloride) is but one of many such compounds which are found in water.

Sediment. Fragmental mineral material transported or deposited by water or air.

Self-supplied industrial use. Water supply developed by an individual industry or factory for its own use.

Specific yield. The amount of water that can be obtained from the pores or cracks of a unit volume of soil or rock.

Structure (in soil). Relation of particles or groups of particles which impart to the whole soil a characteristic manner of breaking; some types are crumb structure, block structure, platy structure, columnar structure.

Transpiration. The process by which water vapor escapes from the living plant and enters the atmosphere.

Watershed or drainage area. An area from which water drains to a single point; in a natural basin, the area contributing flow to a given place or a given point on a stream.

Water table. The top of the zone of saturation in the ground.

Weathering. Decomposition, mechanical and chemical, of rock material under the influence of climatic factors of water, heat, and air.

Water Equivalents

1 cubic foot per second (cfs) = 450 gallons per minute, or 7 1/2 gallons per second

1 cfs for 1 day, or 1 cfs-day = about 2 acre feet

1 acre foot = 326,000 gallons

1 cubic foot weighs 62.4 pounds

1 cubic foot = 7 ½ gallons

1 gallon = 8.33 pounds

1 ton = 240 gallons